FRESH FIRE

FRESH FIRE

by MARIO MURILLO

*When You are Finally Serious
About Power in the End Times*

ANTHONY DOUGLAS PUBLISHING
3380 Green Meadow Drive
Danville, CA 94506

Contents

Foreword

FRESH FIRE is a book about an urgent crisis, an awesome opportunity, and a mighty end-time experience with God.

The crisis is in the charismatic/Pentecostal movement. This movement has dominated worldwide evangelism for virtually all the 20th century. The truth of the baptism in the Holy Spirit has unleashed the greatest awakening man has ever known.

This book is not cynical nor caustic in its efforts to expose what I call fatal attractions. I love this precious movement of the Spirit; that is why I must speak out. Silence merely condones her demise.

Overseas, Pentecost thrives mainly because the truth of being rekindled has been seized. Any open-hearted preacher who has visited these foreign revivals comes home to a painful conclusion: we are the weak, carnal, waning version of the worldwide Holy Ghost movement.

Consider this illuminating, personal experi-

ence. I met the greatest living American charis-
matic/Pentecostal evangelist and found him to be
a marvelous man. Yet, when I gently raised questions about American charismatics, he bristled
defensively, his countenance changed completely,
and he rejected out-of-hand any hint of problem
within charisma.

Are we a movement that cannot even entertain the fact of our deep need? Is this not in itself
a clear symptom of our danger?

FRESH FIRE is also about stunning oppor-
tunities. I call these *flash points of the future.*
Communism has collapsed like a house of cards,
leaving millions open to the gospel. Here at home
a wretched vacuum consumes millions of our
youth, yet this very vacuum itself can be a monumental catalyst to awakening.

Finally, this book is a guide to fresh baptisms
in the Holy Spirit. I mean it! There awaits us
new drenchings of holy power, power that will
more than match the flood of evil in this final
moment of mankind.

Satan, sensing impending doom, has broken
into a sprint. He is submerging America as fast
as possible in despair, violence and filth.

But God will deposit a far surpassing tidal
wave of righteouness, boldness, joy, and wisdom
on his willing children.

This is not one more "bless me quick" ditty;

this is a book for those who would thrive amid last days insanity. This is for those who would cry out from an undivided heart, "God, drench me in apathy-killing, fear-destroying, devil-busting fresh fire!"

PART I

CHAPTER ONE

This Present Weirdness:
The Fatal Attraction of Arrogance

Every awakening has a key moment in its life cycle when it dies out or is cleansed and launched afresh.

The symptoms of a revival's death are often very evident to everyone but to those involved in it. It is this penchant for arrogant denial that exacerbates the demise of any awakening.

Jonathan Edwards said of spiritual pride, "Spiritual pride is very apt to suspect others; whereas an humble saint is most jealous of himself, he is so suspicious of nothing in the world as he is of his own heart."[1]

There never was a revival that had the impact of the charismatic/Pentecostal movement of the 20th Century. No other outpouring in history touched more nations, won more souls or so profoundly changed people as this movement which taught the baptism in the Holy Spirit with speaking in tongues.

This Holy Ghost movement in the West, however, is threatening to self-destruct. It may become the revival which shattered and splintered the fastest and spawned the greatest number of heresies and abuses in the shortest period of time.

Do you feel like I do, the awful sense of a heavy heart and a knot in your stomach when you survey the littered landscape of much of the charismatic/Pentecostal movement?

How tragic it was in the late 80's when key evangelists were exposed for moral and financial failure. Sadder still was that pride kept us from seeing the correcting Hand of God on all of us.

Many just blamed Satan and the media, refusing to realize that spiritual pride brought this disaster upon us.

While some of the most visible were guilty of a double life and shunning accountability, we must plead mercy because the arrogance that blinded them runs throughout the movement. Like us, they were simply caught up in the whirl-wind of pride that has enveloped charisma in America.

This is not the time to judge any brother and be ourselves likewise guilty. This is the time to speak in fear and trembling and with tears!

Pride has come in and darkened our view of ourselves. Arrogance makes us forget our responsibility to provide all things honest (II Corinthians 8:21). Pride blinds us to how our leaders must be aboveboard in the eyes of the unsaved (I Timothy 3:7). Pride can even seduce us to bear animosity toward the very ones we want to reach!

How wrong it is for us as leaders not to answer the world's justifiable questions about our finances. Our attitude has been, "This is none of your business, you secular, humanist devils."

Many concerned saints write me and wonder that not only have we not learned our lessons, we now have a new crop of televangelists that seem worse than ever!

My mail is replete with sincere, horrified believers who can't stand certain preachers on television. They ask, "Why do they have to have those bizarre facial contortions?" as they allegedly prophesy. "Why is every Bible verse bent so that it relates only to giving to their ministry?"

It broke my heart to hear of charismatics who changed husbands and wives to find their "real" partner because of a teaching on "soul mates."

It hurts me when I hear how personal prophecy has been abused to the point that in some cases it resembles charismatic horoscopes. Pride, like cocaine, deceives its victims into overconfidence. Pride makes us focus on one pet doctrine and ride it into the ground. Too many of us go from one emotional high to another until now we too closely resemble the New Age movement.

Pride lets us overlook the fact that the charismatic/Pentecostal movement is fractured and deeply divided. Pride goads preachers to sue each other and even pursue press coverage.

Pride and need for respectability have seduced a host of classical Pentecostal churches to abandon their roots. They allow no free worship, no manifestations of the gifts of the Spirit. They revel in a formality that would make an archtraditionalist drowsy. Some of these are former powerhouses that are still dearly loved.

This present weirdness reveals a movement adrift and in decline. In some segments of the movement even our physical appearance is revealing. Empty buildings and repossessed property stand whispering like a shell on the beach where something used to live. Why should so many refuse to even consider that something is wrong?

Our feeble attempts to conjure up excitement are hollow. People shout spiritual warfare buzz words in fantasy fervor . . . no real impact, just harmless shouting. We tilt at windmills instead of real enemies, like so many Don Quixotes.

Once we were a compelling, effective army; once we won souls like nobody else in history. Now a blinding, self-congratulating arrogance is spreading atrophy through previously strong limbs.

The classic prayer in II Chronicles 7:14 begins with "If my people will humble themselves . . ."

Too many of our preachers strut across stages like obnoxious roosters; too many of our words draw attention to ourselves. All of this indulgence must stop; we must wake up to our true state.

In prayer I cried, "Oh, God! I humble myself. Please empower us again by your mercy!" But my heart warns me that unless we do humble ourselves, Jesus will have to give our opportunity to another movement.

CHAPTER TWO

All Dressed Up and Nowhere to Go: The Fatal Attraction of Hoarding Blessings Meant for Others

If there is one imperative in my life, it is winning souls to Jesus Christ. No matter how many souls I might have won, it is never enough. If I stop bringing people to the Lord or stop bearing fruit, God has the right to cut me off and put someone else behind the pulpit.[2]

Esther had it all; her God-given beauty and spirit distinguished her from thousands of young women. God's plan elevated her to become queen.

The threat of holocaust of the Jews was God's key purpose for her promotion. Ironically, the tools given her for deliverance were also the touchstones of her greatest temptation.

Imagine her sitting in the royal penthouse

9

brushing her marvelous hair. She scans the room and takes in the view: a vast wardroom, untold wealth, and servants who wait to fulfill her every whim.

WHAT she *had* could very easily seduce her to forget *WHY* she had it. In other words, she could be all dressed up with nowhere to go.

WHAT and WHY are two words that hold life and death. When you live by a WHAT, you only see objects and blessings as ends in themselves. WHY is a word that kicks the ends out of our little box and wires us into eternity.

Psalm 103:7 tells us that to Israel, God revealed His *acts* but to Moses He revealed His *ways*. That is the crux of the matter: acts are taken at face value; ways are purposes that deepen a person to see his connection to the past and the future. When you see that connection, your life takes on immense meaning.

WHAT Esther had been given would have faded into obscurity had she not known why she had been given it. A sense of destiny and purpose is at the heart of self sacrifice.

I consider that our present sufferings are not worth comparing with the glory that will be revealed in us.   (Romans 8:18)

Yes, there was danger in Esther's going to the king to plead for the Jews, but there was infinitely greater danger in her remaining silent.

He (Mordecai) sent back this answer: ". . . if you remain silent at this time, relief and deliverance for the Jews will arise from another place, but you and your father's family will perish. And who knows but that you will have come to royal position for such a time as this?"

(Esther 4:13,14)

A vast portion of the charismatic/Pentecostal movement in America is all dressed up with nowhere to go. We are drowning in WHAT for a lack of WHY.

We know what our rights and privileges are. We call ourselves "King's Kids"; we relish our claimed authority over demons and treat the implements of war like toys.

Squandering God-given resources is at the heart of what's wrong with us. Where did we go wrong? Primarily, the avarice of the 80's infected us.

One of the intelligent secular assessments of the 80's was the best-seller CIRCUS OF AMBITION by John Taylor. This book surgically exposed ten years of obscene materialism and ran the gamut of what happened in fashion, banking and government. What was so painful about the book is how it began. It didn't open by relating the ills of Donald Trump or Charles Keating; it began by describing the opulent mansion of an evangelist! Then the author openly wonders how the church, the one agency he supposed could have stood up and rebuked the insanity of the 80's, instead became, in his view, a channel for spreading the disease!

WHAT we have received is the baptism in the Holy Spirit. WHY we received it is buried under a pile of man-created traditions of Christian consumerism. It is frightening to think anyone could be empowered for such a time as this only to hoard it.

But the best example of where we are at this moment is a verse in Second Kings. Four lepers sat starving but they rose up and headed for the Syrian camp. God transformed this twilight trip into the most hilarious invasion in history. God sent a roar into the Syrian camp that melted soldiers' hearts into terror and the enemy ran, leaving a feast totally intact.

These lepers were four of the most unlikely heroes in history except perhaps for the Holy Ghost movement in America. Pentecost, like those lepers, rose out of American poverty and desperateness to visibility.

The lepers reached the camp and found no one, so they began to eat. They buried treasure and put on fancy clothes. This is exactly where too many are now: eating, burying treasure, and dressing up.

Suddenly the voice of godly reason gripped them.

If you were to ask me for the single most precise word for us today, it would be II Kings 7:9:

Then they said to each other, "We're not doing right. This is a day of good news and we are keeping it to ourselves. If we wait until daylight, punishment will overtake us. Let's go at once and report this to the royal palace."

They realized the WHY of this provision and the punishment that would surely come if they hoarded it.

So here is a solemn warning to American Spirit-filled Christians:

(1) We sit in a nation cursed with AIDS, bludgeoned by violence, drowning in crime and godlessness. We must realize that as of now, our witness through the media has been failed amusement parks and Rolex watches. We had better wake up to the reason we are Spirit-filled: *the Holy Ghost is in me for such a time as this*

(2) The power of God within me is not only ABLE but is SUPPOSED to flow out at this time. We must find expression in ministry to America's wounds. If we don't, the movement will die.

Any arrogant assumption that we are still the movement of choice is silly at best and destructive at worst. We have virtually lost the unsaved audience. We are hardly impressing anyone but ourselves.

This is your personal call to fresh fire. The road ahead forks and you must choose your direction. If you choose ease, prepare for emptiness and disappointment. If you choose fire, the cleansing will sting but you will witness the release of power and purpose.

CHAPTER THREE

High Maintenance/Low Impact Converts:
The Fatal Attraction to Superficial Mass Production

They can kill a ministry faster than the combined fury of a moral scandal, an IRS audit and an investigation by "60 Minutes."

Like massive blood loss, these people can inflict a drowsy death. Their effect is the same as the black holes of deep space that suck up everything around them. They will use up a ministry, a leader, even a move of God.

I call them "high maintenance/low impact converts." Because of them, pastors dare not preach past noon. They are the reason leaders burn out. These preemies demand constant care and yield nothing in the way of service. In many charismatic churches, leaders are neglecting prayer, evangelism, and vision as they blindly try to counsel, entertain, and lend life support to this group that never seems to grow out of danger.

They are born arrogant and weak. Imagine that combination! This breed is the product of the 1980's theological genetic engineering. They have never felt the sting of repentance and, therefore, have never experienced true resurrection.

Since they are born with an inflated sense of self-importance, they interpret every scripture and define every experience from a "what can it do for me" attitude.

As they boast of great authority, they crumble at the first wave of adversity. They know of all their biblical rights but none of their responsibilities.

To tickle their ears, leaders have endowed them with disastrous misconceptions: victory is no longer a matter of contending but escaping, and avoiding pain. They wage war in a "Sesame Street" fantasy world and dismiss any challenge of life with the collective cry of "I don't receive it."

High maintenance/low impact types run the gamut. They range from the cold, nominal charismatic whose murky concept of God's love rationalizes drinking, occasional indiscretion, feeble worship and sporadic church attendance to the wild fire, commuter charismatic who yells and froths at "bless me, teach me" extravaganzas.

Their common bond is that they are users, not givers. Their fickleness has leaders in a panic, running to keep them distracted. These brats call pastors at all hours for even trivial problems until the leader collapses.

They have no thirst for depth, no long-term commitment, no faith beyond feeling, and no sense of mission to a hurting world. The thought of denying self to grow and be equipped to touch others is like quantum physics to them.

Their unanimous condition is leanness of soul. This was the judgment of God on the Israelites in the wilderness.

They soon forgot His works; they did not wait for His counsel, but lusted exceedingly in the wilderness, and tested God in the desert. And He gave them their request, and sent leanness into their soul. (Psalm 106:13–15 NKJ)

Modern charisma stands guilty of those same four wilderness sins:

(1) We forgot the miracles that birthed our movement
(2) We didn't wait for His counsel
(3) We lusted in the wilderness

(4) We were finally given our request but pro-
     duced converts with leanness of soul

The current crop, garbed in their high-sounding confessions of power, are critically lean of
soul.

There is no foundation there to build a soldier.
The normal immune system that fends off disease
is missing. For all their confident boasts, these
weakened warriors dare not wander beyond
the barracks. True combat would be their imme-
diate undoing.

Worse yet, because they are the darlings of
our movement, we do not see their destructive
impact.

We see ministries stagnating; leaders know
they are exhausted. America is not listening to us
anymore. Our sermons, which are largely harmless talks, are continually being crafted and
tooled into even less threatening self-help talks
that further foment egotistic charisma.

To be sure, we pray! We blame the devil and
accuse the secular humanists. We believe the lack
of money is the root of all evil. We frantically
search for the cause of our depletion while right
under our nose this "parasite" attitude consumes
all that is precious.

The 80's message that created
high maintenance/low impact converts

Millions of people rushed into the Pentecostal/charismatic movement from the late 60's to the mid-80's.

We were an innocent, compelling phenomenon. I was in Los Angeles during what must be remembered by many as a golden age. It was 1969 and in the Shrine Auditorium, Jesus wrought astounding miracles by the hand of Kathryn Kuhlman. Every month for a decade, it was standing room only!

What a presence of God followed that woman! These were meetings with violent miracles in an atmosphere of dignity. Now we have violent meetings but few miracles. All who believe today that they have inherited her mantle should be quiet! There are still many of us who remember her anointing.

David Wilkerson was preaching at the Melodyland Theatre every month at this same time. He spoke as a prophet to the lost youth of Los Angeles. There were nights when 1,000 souls were mightily converted. The conviction that accompanied his preaching was thick and wonderful. It seemed the whole of southern California was swirling with outreach, power, and an infectious simplicity and joy.

But this charged atmosphere was by no means

limited to Los Angeles. Similar reports of power covered America.

The preaching of that time was demanding. The sinner was accosted by love and fire and directed to change now and change totally.

Against the backdrop of power and glory, preachers could be demanding. Obeying God in this atmosphere seemed reasonable; radical change followed automatically.

As stated before, every revival movement reaches a point where original fire wanes to a flicker. What is done at this time is crucial to the awakening's future.

What we should have done was repent and plead for the fire to be restored. My contention is that, like Samson, we "wist not that the Spirit of God" had left so many of our projects.

Healthy awakenings change the secular culture around them. Weakened movements begin to absorb surrounding cultural trappings.

The message we began to preach in the 80's was born of double panic: dwindling crowds and the need to compete with American greed.

Too many of our leaders were intimidated by the 80's selfishness. They began preaching as revelation a message that was nothing more than scripturized Wall Street.

The 80's tumor was believing you can have it all and get it without effort. A nation gorged itself on pleasure without responsibility, excellence without exertion, and expression without restraint.

What this lie did to America is beyond calculation. The family is a war-ravaged refugee; public school is a nightmare; the U.S. is so violent that no nation on earth approaches her capacity for mayhem.

Many 80's preachers will answer for not only not rebuking that insane decade but for echoing the madness.

Herc is a distillation of the teaching that fetched an entire generation to a synthetic faith:

(1) God wants you to have it all now.
(2) You are instant royalty and, therefore, immediately entitled to authority, power gifts, and profuse blessing.
(3) Don't let Satan rob you of your joy, finances, or anything.
(4) Rebuke adversity; don't receive it.

Now observe the basic tenets of early charismatic/Pentecostals:

(1) You have been snatched from eternal damnation to show forth the praises of Him who called you out of darkness.
(2) Your body belongs to Jesus; be a living

sacrifice. This is reasonable service because you were bought with a price. Crucify the works of the flesh daily.

(3) The baptism of the Holy Spirit has been given to you to be a witness and to fulfill the great commission.

(4) Live modestly, vigilantly, and in constant prayer and fellowship because of end-time darkness and because your true reward will be in heaven.

When you contrast these two sets of values, it is easy to see what kind of person each produces.

One is selfish, turned in, looking for more candy from God. The other is sober, gratefully serving Jesus as lord, and strong in faith.

One is addicted to feelings and flattering leaders. The other is low maintenance, standing in God and reproducing other strong disciples.

The poisoned leader

To have poisoned preaching, you must have a poisoned preacher. What infected many charismatic preachers was their need for a crowd at any cost and the intensity of America's cultural sin.

Today we have traveling seminar teachers. Some are good and their contribution is valid;

others simply purvey a snake oil, quick-fix illusion.

They make wild promises of instant words from God and shortcuts to overcoming life and gaining financial abundance.

All of these miracles will come in a single day of training. Their pitch is classic: have it by to-day; find the missing ingredient; take the short-cut that will jump-start your blessing. But what is the catalyst to ignite their secret ingredient? It is almost always a donation to the teacher. These men are poisoned by greed.

So naive are the students that they don't even bother to ask where the money is going. The teacher will say, "It doesn't matter, just give in faith." But it does matter! If you plant in good soil, you will reap a return but indiscriminate sowing shows that you are only concerned about getting a return, not worship or meeting a need.

There are other kinds of venom that over-power leaders. Pastors can be just as misguided as anyone. Some, in fact, are poisoned with an inordinate love for their congregation. I am not referring to sexual misconduct but a desperate need for popularity. Their preaching is designed solely to sustain hero worship.

The shepherd indulges himself in a euphoria of being wanted and needed. He wants them to like him; he loves them because they love him. He is over-protective until he is even protecting the people from God and insulating them from rightful changes that would require service.

Richard Lovelace described this pitiful tendency: "It becomes tacitly understood that the laity will give pastors places of special honor in the exercise of their gifts, if the pastors will agree to leave their congregations' pre-Christian life-styles undisturbed and do not call for the mobilization of lay gifts for the work of the kingdom. Pastors are permitted to become ministerial superstars. Their pride is fed and their insecurity is pacified even if they are run ragged, and their congregations are permitted to remain herds of sheep in which each has cheerfully turned to his own way."[3]

The people of these worship centers remain in incubators. They are weak and addicted to the pastor's approval.

Another unseen villain is an abuse in the church growth movement. Leaders are intoxicated with church size as the end-all goal of life.

Pastors are fed refried sociology that mitigates against true evangelism. Instead of weeping over cities to inherit God-given strategies, they sit in seminars and salivate over the latest techniques and buzz words meant to increase numbers.

In observing this heartbreaking tendency, Jack Hayford said, "I am aware that 'Church Growth' is a more popular term than 'Evangelism' and

I'm aware that 'marketing' is more contemporary than 'evangelizing'."

Tragically and ironically, many ideas put forth today that are meant to cause growth will reap decline and jeopardize the number of souls that can be saved in a city.

Once you get on the merry-go-round of using "sharp programs" to attract and hold crowds, you are at the mercy of vicious competition. Churches and leaders become crushed under the demands of fickle saints who will transfer to your church to give you a shot at entertaining them better than the last guy did. People are conditioned to pit one church's perks against another. We used to produce people who were committed because they were smitten by power and joy and felt assigned to a congregation by the Holy Spirit.

It is dangerous when a church combines psychology, salesmanship, and "Tonight Show" tactics to build a large church. Dangerous because they actually perceive themselves as a factor for awakening when they may be only a decoy.

Satan will gladly concede into any city an impotent commuter church of even thousands. This group is no threat to take a city. They run on human fuel. They are in a church almost solely for escape or amusement.

How can they possibly grasp war? How can they ever be trained to attack?

The charismatic movement is far from dead but we are equally far from health.

A noted physician confided to me about an impending disaster in the American health services system. He said that all the infants that are born addicted to crack cocaine or infected with the AIDS virus are draining billions each year in medical costs and personnel. The system, in fact, may collapse because of them.

This is a brutal analogy but, nonetheless, I believe it must be applied. For every poorly converted, self-absorbed, weak and addicted baby we produce in the American charistmatic/Pentecostal movement, we must create vast life support systems and divert time and talent to keep him alive.

Because self-centered converts don't reproduce, they will shrink our numbers. Because leaders won't confront them, the strong and committed among us will become disheartened.

As a spiritual force, we are doomed to continued decline until we fade into the archives of revival has-beens.

What must be done to create low maintenance, high impact converts? The answer begins with fresh fire on leaders! Fire that will burn out the juvenile need for human recognition. Fire that will consume the intimidation of American culture. Fire that will engulf carnal infiltrations wherever and whenever they appear.

Let the flames rise till we recall that the timeless person of Christ is the most magnetic force we will ever release on a decadent society.

Satan may unveil a new social craze each year but it is utterly futile against the anointing. He knows that; God help us to know it.

Fire-born prayer will arm us with weapons for the present darkness. Let those who lead us confront the hypocrite and, when necessary, prune the crowd back to Gideon's 300 who will take the city. Let's empty church boards of manipulating men who exchange money for their pernicious influence. But above all, let us produce the true convert!

I sat spellbound as Stanley Jones spoke at the most liberal theological seminary in Berkeley. This giant of God spoke to the most cynical, intellectually smug group I've ever seen. He hit them with love and simplicity even though he was armed with as great a mind as the church has ever known. He defended the reality of the faith of Christ with irresistible precision. "It's the reality of conversion," he said, "the fact that someone can stand and say 'I have been transformed by Jesus.' The personal testimony, that is the word for which there is no retort! With all your books, theories and skepticism, you have no defense against the simple power of a true conversion."

Fresh fire will liberate any leader to thunder

messages that create disciples who will, in turn, create others.

Fire begets fire; compromise begets compromise. Psalm 110:2 says, "Your people will be willing in the day of your power." Above all else, this movement needs to produce a firestorm of willing converts.

CHAPTER FOUR

"Honey, I Shrunk the Devil!": The Fatal Attraction to a Spiritual Warfare Fad

The seven sons of Sceva tried to steal an authority that was not theirs by adding the postscript "in Jesus' name." Their discomfiture by the demon should be a warning to us. In the inevitable clash with the powers of evil arrayed to overthrow the work of God, no assumed authority will avail. Going through the motions is not good enough. Words alone, no matter how religious, have no intrinsic power.[4]

In 1982, a great outpouring of the Spirit came to San Jose, California. Many thousands were impacted in a meeting that was originally scheduled for four nights but exploded into 22 weeks. There were nights of such glory that man's program was unceremoniously dumped by a tidal wave of God's flooding hungry souls.

Key truths surfaced in that visitation. One was that the passivity of the church must be cured. Militancy born of the Spirit was a clear feature of these Christians in the Silicon Valley. Spiritual warfare, a long-neglected area, was being restored to a huge number of God's people.

Simultaneous with the days of power in San Jose, other sections of America were being visited in both spiritual life and the renewed sense of warfare.

During the revival, one night I stood to preach at Calvary Community Church when the Spirit warned me of a coming counterfeit to true spiritual warfare.

I solemnly warned the people that spiritual warfare could become a fad. I had no idea how much worse the abuses would be than what I had imagined.

The most disturbing aspect of this spiritual warfare fad is a *trivial view of Satan*. We dare not view him as a toy who will flee because of some nifty phrase we shout.

Exotic procedures and extra-scriptural tactics are spouted effortlessly. Take, for example, the theory (quite absent from scripture) that after you discover the name of the regional demon that controls your area, you must then go to where the spirit revealed his stronghold and yell at him. Others began telling churches that they needed to receive their "warfare tongue."

Still others leased a jet to circle over Southern California to break the "power of the air." They called it "clearing the air."

A book by a California pastor claimed that this warfare-type prayer had "cleared the skies" over Dallas. Tragically, by the end of that same year Dallas had more policemen shot and killed than any city in America.

This sad illustration is only one disturbing example of a seriously mistaken view of real victory over Satan.

If our view of the world is from the ease and insulation of the sanctuary, we can be totally blind and bereft of true authority, true spiritual strategies and impact.

Chuck Girard, Dony McGuire and Reba Rambo have written true battle hymns for the church but too many charismatic centers now feast on a series of "Devil, you're a punk and we're going to get you" choruses and actually make this their total worship. Some can get so hyped when a pure worship chorus (one that exalts the Lord and doesn't mention Satan) is sung, they actually feel let down.

The true spiritual giants of history revealed their mettle by being the blazing conscience of a community. They pressed the battle where it really mattered, and abolished the works of darkness that cleaned up cities. To them we would look like silly children with styrofoam swords.

Where is the proof of all this alleged damage we've supposedly done to Satan? How dare we pass off arrogant posturing and "war games" as true spiritual authority!

There is no mystery to why personal holiness is not a priority to these weekend warriors. They have bought into the lie that authority is confessed based on our justification in Christ when, in fact, authority over Satan is imparted to the vessel who has proven character.

Real Victory from Real Authority

While we recognize one war in the spiritual world, the Bible speaks of three: (1) our flesh (2) the world (3) Satanic power. We must obtain victory on all three fronts, not just one. To lose in one arena is to lose in all.

Certain purveyors of spiritual warfare can totally neglect their soul because they don't recognize the war between self and Christ. You can't win against Satan until you win against the unChristlike attitudes that freely infect us.

Self is a forgotten foe in charisma. While we scream about nebulous attacks on the works of darkness, that villainous spy works unhindered. While some boast of great victories, the fact of their actual defeat is evident daily in coarse joking, sporadic hard drinking, lifestyle addiction, and selfish ambition disguised as vision.

If we have not won in the arena of self and have not conquered the encroachments of the world, we dare not mess with Satan.

If Satan wanted to, he could effortlessly penetrate the Reynolds Wrap armor and Mattel toy weapons that so many trust in. In a real satanic assault, they would be sent running for their lives like the sons of Sceva who made exorcism a game.

The fact that Satan hasn't openly attacked has to do with a deeper evil! While he might relish exposing the fantasy might of these believers, he gains more by letting thousands stomp, kick, scream, and carry on, harmlessly distracted from the real work of God.

In Acts 8, Philip the evangelist settled the question of how to win a city once and for all.

The New Age village he entered boasted a great sorcerer who had amazed from the least to the greatest. Philip didn't search for the ruling demon's name; he proclaimed the Name that is above all names!

Philip went down to a city in Samaria and proclaimed the Christ there. When the crowds

*heard Philip and saw the miraculous signs he
did, they all paid close attention to what he said.
With shrieks, evil spirits came out of many, and
many paralytics and cripples were healed. So
there was great joy in that city.*   (Acts 8:5–8)

Proclaiming Christ broke demonic power. The
weapon of choice, was, is, and always will be
the gospel thrust forth by a vessel fully armed,
who has victory on three fronts. Like David, they
killed the lion of their flesh, the bear of the
world, before they ventured out to Goliath,
the giant.

To get charisma from the playground to
the battleground will not be an easy task. But the
fantasy is wearing thin and many believers are
asking disturbing questions about the pep rallies
they have attended.

The shouts of superiority over the devil have
not translated into real victory in daily life.
Moreover, they, unlike some "state of the art"
preachers, live in a real world where violence
is increasing, abortion abounds, and immorality is overwhelming.

It is time to discard the hollow boast of
"Honey, I shrunk the devil" and ask God to restore us to the path of real victory, real authority. We cannot say, "The weapons of our warfare
are not carnal" if they are!

We cannot say, "They are mighty to the tearing down of strongholds" if the stuff we use can't tear down strongholds.

And we dare not then ask for the weapons of God. Their first target will be the strongholds of self, which they will home in to blow down long before any thought is given to territorial spirits in your city.

Even Jesus took care to cover this first. "Satan is coming and he has nothing in me."

Just as in every previous kind of extreme in the Charismatic Movement, this one, too, will have its victims. People's faith will be shipwrecked by this naive approach to a very real war.

The Bible Foretold this Abuse

Paul warns of this arrogance in Jude. First, he foretells the blustery boasts of misguided preachers: "For certain men whose condemnation was written about long ago have secretly slipped in among you. They are godless men, who change the grace of our God into a license for immorality and deny Jesus Christ our only Sovereign and Lord." (Jude 4)

Then he exposes their hidden carnal agendas, referring to their derisive language toward Satan: "In the very same way, these dreamers pollute their own bodies, reject authority and slander celestial beings. But even the archangel Michael, when he was disputing with the devil about the body of Moses, did not dare to bring a slanderous accusation against him, but said, 'The Lord rebuke you!' " (Jude 8,9)

A generation cursed those leaders during Vietnam who had underestimated the enemy and sent thousands of our boys to needless early graves.

How will we look back on the frivolous teachers of this moment who claimed to arm people, only to find that Satan will ask, "Jesus I know; Paul I know, but *who are you?*"

As Arthur Mathews said, "For every provocation against God's cause, there is a provision for victory."

There remains for us, then, a victory in the real war and God longs to reveal it. We can be "known in hell." But it comes through authentic prayer from a heart broken to stop evil, a heart that seeks fresh fire.

CHAPTER FIVE

Fratricide:
The Fatal Attraction to Competition

Two men, both visible charistmatic leaders, both accused of immorality, engaged in lawsuits against each other. Not only did they both refuse good counsel but they aired their vendettas through the secular media. All America watched a hideous family fight as neither one listened to Paul's advice to "allow yourself to be defrauded." Seemingly neither was willing to be silent and neither was willing to let God vindicate him. A lifetime of building a ministry was crushed through their war with each other.

I know these men personally. May I tell you that I still believe that both of them are sincere men who were caught up in a spirit that permeates charisma in America?

Before we crucify them for using a secular court, we must look at the value system of an entire movement. We have to examine the vicious competition that is now an integral part of how leaders do business and then we'll grasp how they are driven to this option.

Church government can be motivated by political expedience rather than biblical procedure in bringing correction to a fallen leader.

A buddy system exists that allows the "right" leader in adultery to get off with a slap while the "wrong" leader is discarded and never helped back up.

Wounded preachers feel expendable and, sadly, they take matters into their own hands.

This is only one example of fratricide in the charismatic/Pentecostal movement. Before we look at others, let's get a proper history and definition of fratricide.

While Eve was responsible for our sin nature, it was *Cain* who gave us murder. It is significant that humanity's first bloodshed was brother killing brother . . . fratricide.

History verifies that the most wicked and bloody wars have always been civil wars. Small wonder, then, that Satan is called the "accuser of the breathren" or that Proverbs targets as one of the Lord's supreme points of wrath "those who sow discord between brothers."

What fratricide does is kill faster and wider than any other kind of hate. First, because no hate burns hotter than the hate born where love once resided. Just ask any divorce attorney or, better yet, talk to anyone who has ever been in a really good church fight. There is simply no fighting like in-fighting.

Jude, verse 4, carries this warning, "Certain men crept in unnoticed." Then Jude adds this warning for us in the end times: "Woe unto them for they have gone in the way of Cain." (verse 11) Are we in the midst of the spirit of Cain that Jude predicted?

I believe this spirit infected us when we began to prize success above integrity. Now more than ever the value of a leader is gauged by the size of his ministry, book and tape sales, and mailing list. Our applause goes to the big and famous, not to the humble and obedient. This has made us a breeding ground for jealousy and competition.

A business man once lamented to a preacher I know what a cutthroat world the business word was and that he could not possibly understand because he was in ministry. My friend laughed and said, "Oh, brother, are you wrong!" When a competitor tries to cut your throat, it's business; when a preacher tries to do it, he tells you, "The Lord told me to do it!"

Now let's look at how fratricide creeps in. Look at the example of a young person who gets saved out of a lurid past. There is a perverse celebrity to what he was before he met Jesus and he is paraded before the church like a trophy, even though scripture clearly warns us not to give responsibility to a novice. Soon there are multiple hurts. First, some other young, sincere preacher, who has been waiting to lead, is punished because he or she doesn't have the notorious testimony. Next, because the real intention is to use the freshly saved treasure out of darkness to get a crowd, he is loved and useful only as long as he draws crowds. He can be destroyed by a horrible empty feeling when he is no longer the hot testimony. They drop out of sight as fratricide seeks out the next crowd draw.

The charismatic movement's policy is to "get them up on the high wire as soon as possible" but we have no safety net, and if they fall, we quickly remove the body so the show can go on.

Another rude awakening for young preachers comes when they see that in many cities leaders regularly conduct turf wars. Itinerant preachers must carefully maneuver a battlefield of politics. To befriend one pastor makes you the enemy of another. Too often a leader comes up through the ranks, forced to succeed by compromising his personal Christian convictions.

Most preachers begin as innocent, willing vessels but are soon subjected to those shocking, disillusioning experiences. They find anger everywhere. Character assassination is pandemic.

Have you met a leader who has been in ministry for years and still exudes the sweet love of Jesus? Or one who has a positive attitude of cooperation? Mark that leader, for he is a greater miracle than Lazarus!

If a leader has faced our current fratricide and is still ungrieved in spirit, it is because a mountain of prayer and discipline went into maintaining a right spirit. Every significant pastor I've ever met has a common greatness: an ability to take insults to the Lord. They possess a skill to stay positive against a tide of cruelty against themselves and their loved ones. They have weathered a violent sea of betrayal, gossip, and competition, and have learned to expect it from the least expected sources.

In some Spirit-filled denominations, professional competition is so crushing that our leaders can't confess their sins to each other, because rather than weep and help, a rival pastor will use the information to remove the competition. Early on, sins could be caught and disaster prevented; instead, they fester until the fear of being caught can no longer hold back the emptiness of their life and drives them into immorality.

Leaders need friends, not fans. Their worth as people must not be based on crowds or any trappings of success.

Can we face it? This once humble, spontaneous charismatic renewal, once so significant, now appears to many to be a mean-spirited machine of competition where people are expendable.

What a rebuke it is when you see that Mormon evangelists never criticize each other publicly. The cults can sit down and strategize a citywide impact while we are at war against each other.

Fratricide is a major reason the anointing eludes us. How can we bear the ultimate message of love, forgiveness, and restoration when our approach to one another violates everything the gospel represents?

Can you blame the young preacher who gets discouraged by the warlord mentality of leaders that cut up a city and mark off their territory?

And while we are on the subject of territories, consider this great irony: one of today's most popular teachings is on "territorial spirits." This theory holds that a ruling demon controls cities and regional areas. To release blessing, this ruling demon must be bound.

What if the ruling spirit isn't a demon at all but "territorial charismatic leaders" who bind Christ from touching the city?

Can you now feel for the pastor of a small work who sees all the attention and resources go to those whose results feed the success cult and render his own vital work meaningless?

The "brother against brother" spirit has done as much damage as any other fatal attraction in the Body of Christ. No wonder we can't take cities; too many of our leaders get their thrills from carnal business approaches to ministry.

But worst of all is that when brothers disagree, they are too proud to follow scripture and sit down and talk to each other. Jonathan Edwards warned of pride that grips leaders during disagreements. Listen to his timeless counsel:

". . . spiritual pride takes great notice of opposition and injuries that are received, and is apt to be often speaking of them, and to be much in taking notice of their aggravations, either with an air of bitterness or contempt."[5]

God help us to start talking to each other! God help us to see any wounds we inflict on brothers! God help us to control our tongue.

This fatal attraction is ugliest to the Lord because, as I said before, conflicting, Cain-like leaders force sheep to choose sides. Fratricide always has many innocent victims and their blood, like Abel's, cries to God from the ground.

This great evil will stop charisma cold! We need a baptism of brotherly love, a fiery cleansing that will burn away this cancer from the movement.

CHAPTER SIX

The Adonijah Factor:
The Fatal Attraction to Hype

Adonijah almost destroyed Israel by preventing the coronation of Solomon.

A golden era of prosperity and wisdom was nearly aborted by the self-promoting scheme of one of David's sons.

How did it happen? By a void created by David's advancing age and his procrastination in advancing Solomon to the throne.

When King David was old and well advanced in years, he could not keep warm even when they put covers over him. (I Kings 1:1)

Now Adonijah, whose mother was Haggith, put himself forward and said, "I will be king." So he got chariots and horses ready, with fifty men to run ahead of him. (I Kings 1:5)

Verse six of this chapter answers the question of why this young man was bent toward evil: "His father had never interfered with him by asking, 'Why do you behave as you do?' He was also very handsome and was born next after Absalom."

The young man's marketing skills were impressive. First he gathered leaders who had power but were disgruntled with David. "Adonijah conferred with Joab son of Zeruiah and with Abiathar the priest, and they gave him their support." (I Kings 1:7)

Then he cleverly avoided men of integrity who might expose him.

But Zadok the priest, Benaiah son of Jehoiada, Nathan the prophet, Shimei and Rei, and David's special guard did not join Adonijah.

(I Kings 1:8)

The silence of David and the people's yearning for dynamic leadership made them easy prey for Adonijah. A great ceremony with multiple thousands ensued.

Adonijah then sacrificed sheep, cattle and fattened calves at the Stone of Zoheleth near En Rogel. He invited all his brothers, the king's sons, and all the men of Judah who were royal officials.

(I Kings 1:9)

The central hero of this story who, more than anyone else, stopped the madness was Nathan. He immediately went to David's wife and Solomon:

Then Nathan asked Bathsheba, Solomon's mother, "Have you not heard that Adonijah, the son of Haggith, has become king without our lord David's knowing it? Now then, let me advise you how you can save your own life and the life of your son Solomon. Go in to King David and say to him, 'My lord the king, did you not swear to me your servant: "Surely Solomon your son shall be king after me, and he will sit on my throne"? Why then has Adonijah become king?' . . ." (I Kings 1:11–13)

Many in Judah had assumed David was aged and incompetent; others has interpreted his silence during Adonijah's campaign as an endorsement.

What few realized was the true constitution of David. Old? Yes. Tired? Very. Weak? Completely. But they said the only words that could ignite him . . . the kingdom is at stake!

King David said, "Call in Zadok the priest, Nathan the prophet and Benaiah the son of Jehoiada." When they came before the king, he said to them: "Take your lord's servants with you

*and set Solomon my son on my own mule and
take him down to Gihon. There have Zadok the
priest and Nathan the prophet anoint him king
over Israel. Blow the trumpet and shout, 'Long
live King Solomon!' Then you are to go up with
him, and he is to come and sit on my throne and
reign in my place. I have appointed him ruler
over Israel and Judah."*   (I Kings 1:32–35)

The vacuum was filled and the nation saved.
The release of joy was complete.

*Zadok the priest took the horn of oil from the
sacred tent and anointed Solomon. Then they
sounded the trumpet and all the people shouted,
"Long live King Solomon!" And all the people
went up after him, playing flutes and rejoicing
greatly, so that the ground shook with the sound.*
                                        (I Kings 1:39,40)

What on earth does this bit of history have to
do with the fatal attraction of the American Holy
Ghost movement? In short . . . everything.

It is indescribably urgent for us to see the Adonijah factor at work in our movement.

Adonijahs will arise whenever a void of authority exists. The David's of this past generation,
the anointed, mighty men and women of God
are old.

Like Adonijah, a host of new voices have promoted themselves. They have leased kingly-looking horses to run before them and have retained the services of publicity agencies. They claim that the mantle of some true departed lion of God has fallen on them.

Have you seen these preachers who have such an air of pride they seem like they are strutting even when they are sitting down? The reason they thrive and we tolerate them is because of this void of power in the movement. We are between revivals and it is hard to remember the real fire of God.

These modern Adonijahs carry the same capacity for disaster as the original. Specifically, the danger is that the charistmatic/Pentecostal movement for the first time is capable of being overrun by leaders who are self-promoted and not divinely called.

The five-year period from 1947 to 1952 saw one of the earth's most significant expressions of power. Not only did Israel become a nation in that period, but many great men and women of God—such as Billy Graham, Oral Roberts and Kathryn Kuhlman—were raised up and mightily used by the Lord.

But the roar of spiritual giants is not in the land today as it once was. The glaring spiritual void which exists in America is caused by the scarcity of apostles, prophets, and evangelists who are not in ministry for the money, the power, the public attention or the acclaim.

Unfortunately, they persuade many to follow them. But if one looks closely, Adonijahs can easily be recognized: they peddle their truth. Without marketing and promotion, they have no substance and flavor, no vitality, no compelling message and no solution to the evil of the day.

The real horror isn't that there are counterfeit or carnal preachers; we've always had them. The difference is that now for the first time they are mainstream and operate almost unchallenged. Whereas reason and discernment once relegated the spurious preacher and the extremists to the periphery, they now draw large crowds and enjoy acceptance, partly because the elders of this movement are silent and procrastinate in promoting the truly anointed new voices. But many will use the scripture in Proverbs (". . . a man's gift will make room for him and place him before kings . . .") to defend a view that real gifts of God are promoted, no matter what.

But the key to this verse is that it will place *him before kings*. It is vital, then, for that king to release the gift to the people.

To be sure, our Old Testament story verifies the awesome danger of a king sleeping when he should be promoting. But how can we confront

the Adonijahs of our day without looking judg-
mental? You can even suspect Mario here of sour
grapes. Believe me, I have painfully mulled that
over and over again in my spirit. I refused to
write this chapter until I knew it could be done
in love and by the will of God.

My motive is Nathan's motive: a great work of
God is threatened. Am I jealous of Adonijahs?
No! Our crusades overflow; we are in a hurri-
cane of opportunity. Even as I write this, we are
laying the groundwork for a mighty world outreach headquarters near San Francisco.

My heartbreak is over the central honor that
hype and emotional frenzies now enjoy. My grief
is over the garish, fleshly displays that are
palmed off as manifestations of God.

Do you get a little queasy when well-known
evangelists blow on people so they'll fall down?
Do you feel embarrassed when they "shoot blessings" with a pointed finger, sometimes behind
their back and even under their leg?

But there is a source of danger we have not yet
addressed that goes well beyond Adonijah.

*A horrible and shocking thing has happened in
the land: the prophets prophesy lies, the priests
rule by their own authority, and my people love
it this way. But what will you do in the end?*
(Jeremiah 5:30,31)

It must be remembered that Jeremiah was not easy to shock. He had witnessed Judah in her lowest condition. He had decried immorality among leaders and idol worship for years.

For him to employ the words "a horrible and shocking thing has happened" is noteworthy! That's how serious a disaster it is when prophets and priests conspire to manipulate the Word of God. Lies and human authority had silenced the real message from the Lord but the great evil is in the words "my people love it this way."

Charisma in America has a stomach for hype, a fatal attraction to Adonijahs. That is the real danger: People love it this way!

A growing majority of charismatics relish sensational packaging and overlook the absence of a true work of the Spirit.

When the giants of God conducted miracle services, wheelchairs were emptied, cancers vanished, blind eyes opened, and as a side benefit, people went down under the power. Does it seem to you that so-called miracles services now focus on the side benefits? Is it because there are so few medically verifiable miracles? Are all these shenanigans a smoke screen?

Older saints may have a dim memory of those startling meetings of yesterday and the more recently converted have no experience with such meetings at all.

But the older generation has seen the fire and

the glory of God. They know the true miracles of Christ. They are more readily able to discern the difference between gold and fool's gold; the anointing and emotion; and between self-promotion and God-given favor.

Although today a minister's success is gauged by his popularity or by the size of his ministry's budget, the real greatness, David's greatness, was that he repeatedly placed his life on the line for the sake of truth. Godless, carnal experts advise today's preachers to seek the secure and supposedly important life. But no risk, no courage, no vision, and no power are in it.

Satan is not impressed! He hisses at ministries that have the ability to whip up a crowd or boast of great gifts. He knows how pathetic a preacher's efforts are if there is no brokenness there or if there is no authentic work of the cross in him.

Lucifer dismisses our rattling swords made of untempered metal; his mouth waters when he sees the roosters who crow but he reels in horror before eagles commissioned by God.

Adonijahs have neither suffered nor been rebuked. Perhaps their popularity is because they legitimize their audience's need to likewise escape pain and responsibility.

Retirement is not an option for the vessels with God's hand on them. They must have an iron will which says, "Whenever the need arises, whenever the devil rears his ugly head, whenever

demons control the government, whenever public schools and streets become a war zone, and
the fire has left the movement, I'm ready to
spring from my bed and be a lion for God."

I have a dear 77-year-old friend, Vic Munyer,
who has been an usher for Billy Graham Crusades since 1948. In spite of his chronological age,
he's younger than I am. The secret of his youth
is that he refuses to talk about previous moves of
God. He is constantly rising on his elbow and
vowing to be available when the kingdom is
threatened.

After Solomon's coronation, a release occurred
in the nation of Israel.

*. . . All the people came up after him (Solomon),
and the people piped with pipes, and rejoiced
with great joy, so that the earth rent with the
sound of them.* (I Kings 1:40 KJV)

Previously, the people had so fervently wanted
a king, they accepts the prospect of Adonijah as
their new ruler. But it was not a wholehearted,
enthusiastic acceptance.

On the other hand, when Solomon was an-
nounced as King David's successor, the cry from
the people of God was so deafening that it tore
the ground upon which they stood. So will we
roar in festival when right new leadership is
released by the veteran legends of our movement.

Older, established ministries will either ride on the new wave or fade into monumental nostalgia and speak of days gone by. The leaders can look for a charismatic rest home or they can get up on their elbows and say, "I will be on fire as long as I am on this earth! I will be a part of everything God is doing!" Who more than Lester Sumrall and Kenneth Hagin epitomize what I am saying? We still need our Davids to give balance, direction and force.

On the other hand, persons who would be like Solomon should never indulge in self-promotion. They should not attempt to discover politically who is worth knowing, or whom they should emulate. They must rest in the faithfulness of God to wake up a David on their behalf.

. . . Promotion cometh neither from the east, nor from the west, nor from the south. But God . . . putteth down one, and setteth up another."
(Psalm 75:6,7 KJV)

To Solomon, the Lord said, ". . . if thou wilt walk before me, as David thy father walked, in integrity of heart, and in uprightness, to do according to all that I have commanded thee, and wilt keep my statutes and my judgments: then I will establish the throne of thy kingdom upon Israel for ever . . ." (I Kings 9:4,5)

God's blessing is reserved for those committed

to walking according to his Word. The Adonijahs must depend upon their human abilities, but the Davids and Solomons walk in the power of God.

We need a new flame to awaken us to real miracles. Of all the needed applications of fresh fire, this must be the greatest!

To resurrect our sense of what is flesh and what is sacred, we must have a new baptism.

Stop following Adonijahs; quit relying on the hot flash. Never has so little power been marketed as being so great. The movement of the Spirit won't abide our fascination with carnal leaders; it will leap onto an entirely new group that wants reality.

CHAPTER SEVEN

The Future Is Not What It Used to Be: The Fatal Attraction to Worshipping the Past

First Chronicles chapter twelve shows us the warriors that linked hearts with David. Each tribe has its outstanding capability in war.

Men of Issachar, who understood the times and knew what Israel should do—200 chiefs, with all their relatives under their command . . ."
(I Chronicles 12:32)

The ability to read the times is listed here as a weapon. As surely as discernment tends toward victory, so does the lack of it tend toward destruction.

Proverbs warns: without a vision the people

perish. In other words, without an open revelation a movement can die. In Lamentations chapter one, verse nine, the cause of death of the city of Jerusalem is listed as "she did not consider her destiny."

Lot lived in the vexation of Sodom. It finally bent his spirit, dulled his perception and confused his morals. To save the angels of God, he offered his own daughters to the Sodomites. He even had to be persuaded to leave the doomed city.

I've tried so far to show that charisma, like Lot, lies dormant, steeped in American culture and she doesn't see it. We can't seem to stir ourselves to wake up, heed warnings, consider our destiny and discern what we must do.

Jesus wept over Jerusalem:

Now as He drew near, He saw the city and wept over it, saying, "If you had known, even you, especially in this your day, the things that make for your peace! But now they are hidden from your eyes. For the days will come upon you when your enemies will build an embankment around you, surround you and close you in on every side, and level you, and your children within you, to the ground; and they will not leave in you one stone upon another, because you did not know the time of your visitation."

(Luke 19:41–44)

This is no uneventful hour in history. This is our time of visitation.

If even for a moment our eyes could be opened to what they are really doing to our soul and our destiny as a movement, we would recoil from them in horror.

Most of all, our ignorance about events in the near future are keeping us from making urgent changes right now.

Why has God now commanded the Holy Ghost movement to change or be replaced? Something has happened. The time of the Lord's winking at our abuses is over.

There is something about the future that warns us that a new infusion of power must be obtained now. What are those future events and what is it about us that won't let us see the crucial choice we must make now?

Abigail was used in King David's life to remind him of his future just as he was about to forfeit it in an impulsive rage over Nabal.

Please forgive your servant's offense, for the Lord will certainly make a lasting dynasty for my master, because he fights the Lord's battles. Let no wrongdoing be found in you as long as you live. Even though someone is pursuing you to take your life, the life of my master will be bound securely in the bundle of the living by the Lord your God. But the lives of your enemies he will hurl away as from the pocket of a sling. When the Lord has done for my master every good thing he promised concerning him and has appointed him leader over Israel, my master will not have on his conscience the staggering burden of needless bloodshed or of having avenged himself. And when the Lord has brought my master success, remember your servant.

David said to Abigail, "Praise be to the Lord, the God of Israel, who has sent you today to meet me. May you be blessed for your good judgment and for keeping me from bloodshed this day and from avenging myself with my own hands."   (I Samuel 25:28–33)

Esau was condemned in scripture for trading his future for instant gratification.

See that no one is sexually immoral, or is godless like Esau, who for a single meal sold his inheritance rights as the oldest son.

(Hebrews 12:16)

Without insight into the future, we can't know what's at stake. We won't muster the needed motivation to change in order to protect our destiny.

But just knowing we have problems is not nearly enough. Fresh fire becomes even more urgent when you see what's just up ahead. We are in the Valley of Decision. Discerning tomorrow may be the final "make or break" act of the charismatic/Pentecostal revival.

Another grave blind spot is our neglect of world evangelism. This is crucial to our survival! As missionary zeal wanes in the American church, the church in the Orient appears to be inheriting our lamp stand as the seat of world outreach.

We frolic in trivial pursuits as the stage is being set for the greatest evangelistic opportunity in history.

The Lord spoke to Isaiah and described Israel as a vineyard that He had planted to bring forth sweet grapes but when He tasted them, the grapes were bitter.

We were planted in and destined to touch America in her darkest moment. As stated before, we are Spirit filled in a time of AIDS, abortion, drugs, militant sodomy and war. We are to be a balm that will heal at the time of America's worst wounds.

We do good things; we petition Congress; we lie down in front of abortion clinics; we do almost everything but the most clearly effective thing: preach a "signs and wonders" gospel in the mainstream of American life.

I wish we hated abortion, pornography and

sodomy more than we do. I wish we hated them
enough to use the weapons of choice; weapons of
our destiny; weapons that bring real victory.

We've plunged into feverish activity, but not
in the sort born of revelation. We race to false
finish lines. Our zeal is so much ignorance on
fire.

Yet one more disease that binds us is the worship of the past. This bondage is hard to detect
because there seems to be nothing wrong with
honoring past heroes. Our past is great; in fact,
it is illustrious. But our past is not our future nor
is it anything like it. Once we're delivered, we'll
declare that the future is not what it used to be.

When Hezekiah began to reign in Judah and
saw the need of moral awakening, the people
had grossly defiled themselves, incurring the
wrath of God.

He had a strange enemy in his campaign to restore God's blessing to the nation. It was a brass
serpent named Nehustan that was an object of
worship. This was no pagan idol made by some
Philistine; it was the brass serpent made by
Moses. Here was the symbol of an awesome
miracle of God in the wilderness centuries before
which was made by their greatest prophet. Now
the people were burning incense to it!

To move Judah into their future, Hezekiah
literally had to smash this symbol of their past.

Right now large pockets of the Pentecostal/

charismatic movement reel under this very form of idolatry. They worship past vessels and the symbols of what they did. Many are pickled by nostalgia. Memories are becoming formaldehyde.

We can't be enticed to live in an afterglow instead of contending for fresh fire to do a new work.

This attitude refuses to believe that anyone today can be as anointed or holy as those legends were.

To some, admitting that a great new work is in progress seems like disloyalty to these great men and women of God. In fact, the best way to honor their memory is to follow their example, which was their courage to do something new!

Had Moses been alive to see Nehustan's perversion, he would have smashed the idol faster than Hezekiah did! So would the great apostles of Pentecost bring us a stinging rebuke for our "oldies but goodies" mentality if they were resurrected.

What Satan did then, he is doing now: blinding the people of God so thay can't discern a time of change. Comfortable, predictable habits must break to ensure a new wave of anointed ministry and vision. It's a syndrome I call looking for Elijah's body.

The Book of Second Kings, chapter two, records this classic resistance to change. Elijah, the prophet, was being called home. A new name was emerging: Elisha, the servant of Elijah.

Elijah made his fiery exit and Elisha took up his mantle. Elijah's groupies were standing on the other side of the river waiting for their hero to return as he had always done in the past.

The new prophet Elisha appeared, raised the mantle, and struck the waters. The waters parted as they had for the old prophet. The river made no distinction between Elijah and Elisha; the river knew the anointing of God. The groupies were another matter; they wanted Elijah, not God's purposes. Elijah was the past; Elisha was the future.

Elisha asked them, "Where is the God of Elijah?" This question cut to the heart of that generation's problem. They had their designated prophet and they begged Elisha to let them go to look for Elijah's body. They suspected that the Spirit had dropped Elijah on a mountain.

How ridiculous to still go looking for a memory when God has deposited the future right into your hand!

Today there are many fresh young voices. But there is a hideous double standard! We will accept the vanishing Elijahs, warts and all, to their destruction while we refuse to acknowledge the most promising young voices, to their starvation.

Many young evangelists are discouraged by the fact that even before they get to resist the attacks of Satan, they must survive the church. Mighty gifts and callings are being delayed because we want time to search for Elijah's body.

This generation is covered with memorabilia and paraphernalia of an age that God says is over. The final victims will be those trapped in this time warp. They will miss the great times of power just ahead.

Imagine being sidelined by nostalgia as a storm of miracles refreshes America. Our first loyalty must be to what Jesus is doing in our day. That means adapting to new names and faces.

If pastors succumb to the carnal tendency to go for what was a big name in the 80's just to draw a crowd, they run the risk of a dead meeting!

The wise person of God will discern the times. The river has parted again and we are to acknowledge where the God of Elijah is.

Many churches and ministries start out as places of power, then evolve into museums and end up as prison houses. Altars of fire become artifacts, miracles become methods, and people end up powerless.

The point is clear. We must find the mantle, not the body, of the prophet. We aren't seeking Elijah; we are seeking Elijah's God.

This, then, is the time of our visitation! Here

and now is the call to face our utterly helpless state. We must not be blind to both our failure and our opportunity.

This is not a time for silver-tongued rascals, charismatic snake oil or light and airy discernment. We need Ezras! Men who can weep with such ferocious grief that their cries cut us to the heart and jolt us out of the coma of our nominal faith. Let their sobs drown out the seductions of our culture, the amnesia and the blindness that can't see tomorrow and is costing us our destiny.

PART II

CHAPTER EIGHT

Flashpoints of the Future:
The Great American Vacuum

"I rob banks because one of three things will happen: I'll be arrested and get three meals a day and a warm place to sleep; I'll get away with the money; or a cop will kill me and put me out of my misery." — 17-year-old boy from Detroit

The 90's are the time of feeling the emptiness; this is the "morning after." Clinics and therapy centers overflow as millions seek liberation from the multiple addictions they contracted in the 80's.

The verdict for those self-compulsive years is in. We have paid dearly and will continue to pay in loss of family, dignity, and even sanity.

This prodigal decade hollowed us out. When the tide of partying, using people, drugs and arrogant materialism receded, it stole the precious and left a profound vacancy.

Lee Atwater, former Republican party strategist, was the definite success story. By using brutal politics, he rose to wealth, prestige and power that few had ever known.

He commandeered the election of George Bush and confessed later that he worked relentlessly to destroy the reputation of Michael Dukakis.

Then Lee was struck down with brain cancer, a disease that reduced him to living wreckage and eventually took his life. He had no foundation; he was utterly helpless. In his case, tragedy became victory because he was dramatically converted and Jesus Christ has become his whole life.

His words to "Life" magazine articulated as precisely as anyone could where we are right now in America.

"The 80's were about acquiring—acquiring wealth, power, prestige. I know. I acquired more wealth, power and prestige than most. But you can acquire all you want and still feel empty. What power wouldn't I trade for a little more time with my family? What price wouldn't I pay for an evening with friends? It took a deadly illness to put me eye to eye with that truth, but it is a truth that the country, caught up in its ruthless ambitions and moral decay, can learn on

my dime. I don't know who will lead us through the 90's, but they must be made to speak to this spiritual vacuum at the heart of American society, this tumor of the soul."

This is what I call "The Great American Vacuum." The 80's were, in essence, the years of the depraved and the deprived. The depraved invited the bitter nothingness the party leaves while the deprived wallowed in anger because they were never invited to the party. In fact, in the 80's, it became fashionable to resent the poor as underachievers. Yet, nobody is paying more dearly for the 80's than our children. The savings and loan scandal and other travesties of legalized business crime have despoiled their future by loading them with a debt for life.

Another lethal mixture poisons our youth: unbearable despair and pain, combined with a sensual philosophy, fuels their drug abuse.

Television broadcasts a futile anti-drug commercial. An egg is frying and a voice warns, "This is your brain on drugs. Any questions?" Yes! A very big question . . . What do you do with the pain? A pain so severe that a fried brain is considered an improvement! Our youth even wear t-shirts that exclaim, "A mind is a wonderful thing to waste."

Marriage and family are natural protectors of sanity and children in our society. Even this vital social immune system was trashed in the 80's.

America dignified the lies of the radical feminists and gay activists who view the nuclear family as a threat to its progress.

Every facet of American life is being touched by this painful void. It is our supreme national crisis. It will drive us to revival or it will be remembered as our cause of death.

This is why I believe fresh fire is so crucial and why I have hammered away at the question of what the charismatic movement was doing all this time. As I said before, we not only *didn't* rebuke the 80's madness but many of our preachers flavored scripture to justify their own brand of materialistic partying.

Few warned of the inevitable pain, vacuum and debt. Just as the Israelites said to Aaron (see Exodus 32:1), America screamed, ". . . Come, make us gods!" Too many Holy Ghost preachers tragically were only too willing to comply.

And what are we doing now? We are not prophesying to the hollowness of America, because too many believers have to deal with their own vacuum created by their own partying.

We are like lifeguards who can't swim. How can charismatics rescue anyone while their own marriages, emotions and values are sinking in the same sea as secular America?

God sees the pain, the meaninglessness and the victims. He is aware of the millions of children who have been plunged into poverty by the pandemic divorce of an adulterous generation. He cries for the single mother crushed between career and child care. He is touched by the incurable hurt of a whole youth generation, trapped in a maze of fear and abandonment.

Jesus knows the inner cities of America which are occupied and terrorized by drug gangs every bit as much as Kuwait was by Saddam Hussein.

The great American vacuum will not go unanswered by God! He is about to act!

It is time for love to wipe away the tears and pain of a youth generation orphaned by the 80's.

It is time for a new, mighty authority and boldness to ignite the American church to invade the mean streets of America!

This is the time for brave preachers, not slick, entertainer evangelists. It's time for true prophets whose words slay the lies and enflame righteousness.

The Holy Spirit is about to fall on America in a measure unknown in history. This begs a burning question: what condition will charismatics be in when this outpouring of God begins?

Where do you want to be when this deluge of refreshing strikes America? Mired in apathy? Imprisoned in superficial faith?

Will you look on helplessly as others rejoice in mighty exploits of God?

It is not that God doesn't love the charismatic movement. It's simply that He cannot allow us any longer to be a barrier of His blessing.

We are neglecting our calling at a time when the Lord must act to fill this vacuum. He has sent repeated warnings and He cannot, He *will not*, abide our carnal distractions that jeopardize what He wants to do.

Either we will foolishly ignore His warnings and fade as a movement or we will discard our pride and seek that lifesaving dose of FRESH FIRE.

CHAPTER NINE

If I Had Known I Was Going To Live This Long I Would Have Taken Better Care of Myself

Who could have imagined a war with Iraq or the worldwide collapse of communism? How astonishing for me to grow up with the Berlin Wall only to watch it become a speed bump.

An unseen hand has swiped over the international scene and changed everything. All bets are off; the playing field has been leveled.

Seven hundred fifty million people, who just three years ago were denied it, now have access to the gospel. Governments are pleading for missionaries!

Sleepy charisma is being caught flatfooted in the greatest moment of evangelism since the upper room!

Instead of packing to leave, we need to rest up, get fired up, train, and brace ourselves for a mind-boggling harvest.

Ted Turner publicly accused Christians of having a defeatist mentality. He said that because we believe the world will end in fire any day now, we don't work to do anything meaningful and we are Bozos. His assessment, at best, is misguided. His ignorance, however, is frightening since he owns the Cable News Network.

Does Mr. Turner choose to ignore history? No one in history has built more schools, hospitals, universities and social agencies and just flat out relieved more human misery than the workers of the Christian faith. By now we are used to the media bias against the church. Ted's attack, however, was something else. He intimates that the church is the single threat to world peace and the environment. I believe his attitude is the early manifestation of that ideology which will bring the antiChrist to power.

Like all lies, this one seizes on an element of truth. Sadly, there are those who fit Ted Turner's description, people who are victimized by an end-time euphoria because of events in the Middle East.

I can't help but wonder if many books on prophecy are written to cash in on end-time interest. Scripture teaches a unique balance in end-time behavior. I call it being "edge wise," living at the edge of time, fully realizing the imminent return of the Lord, yet being wise to seize the opportunity to glorify God patiently, deliberately, and with excellence.

You and I have both met people who have been smitten by a general malaise as a result of prophecy abuse; they drop out of college; they have no strategy for their lives; everything is on hold, especially marriage and commitment. Some charismatic/Pentecostals remind me of seniors in high school the week before graduation, bodies in the classroom with hearts and minds somewhere else.

Matthew 24 is often bent into a justification for doom and gloom by end-time prospectors. Yet it is here that the instructions are given that should motivate us to prepare for war and victory.

In verse 6 we see the command that we are not to be troubled:

And you will hear of wars and rumors of wars. See that you are not troubled; for all these things must come to pass, but the end is not yet.
(Matthew 24:6 NKJ)

We are to keep moving forward in the face of headlines. Then in verse 14 we see that the great hope of worldwide harvest is clearly spelled out:

*And this gospel of the kingdom will be preached
in all the world as a witness to all the nations,
and then the end will come.*   (Matthew 24:14 NKJ)

Recently I was in a convenience store and saw
a beer-bellied man wearing a worn-out t-shirt
which was stretched to the maximum. On the
t-shirt were these words: "If I had known I was
going to live this long I would have taken better
care of myself."

The great lament of the charismatic movement may very well be summed up in these
words: "If we had known the rapture was going
to take this long, we would have taken better
care of our walk with God and our vision for the
lost." The great events of the near future may fall
out completely differently than the doomsayers
proclaim. Instead of America declining, she may
be promoted to an expanded role in world leadership. There could actually be peace and a
resulting access to many formerly closed societies.

Because the Vietnam spirit seems to have finally fallen off of America, we will likely regain the
self-confidence needed to accept this new era of
leadership. A dramatic change also seems likely
in the morale of the American worker. For years
American products have been berated. We ourselves have been some of the loudest critics of
both our work force and our youth. Then our
products and our soldiers performed admirably

in the Gulf War. Patriotism jumped way up afterward and we finally seem to be waking up from the media enhanced self-doubt of the previous 15 years.

Do not misunderstand me. I am not touting an American millennium. The road ahead will be hard. What I am saying is that the future is charged with opportunity. This is the worst time to be caught with our head in the sand. This is the most urgent time for the church to recruit young preachers. Bible schools should be overflowing! Missions works should be on red alert to seize the open borders that are even now upon us.

God wants to give us excellence and clout in business, education and government, but we can't see it. The Lord could write a country and western song to the church: "How can I use you while you've got leavin' on your mind?"

I believe fresh fire is the only experience that will save us from squandering this vital moment in history. The whole point to being Spirit filled is to have power to witness.

Earlier I said that teaching trends have moved us away from our commission to a global witness and that the Lord is sternly warning us to seek Him or forfeit our right to lead the next attack. We need this baptism to see the toll that has been taken on our ability to correctly detect the voice of Jesus. There awaits us spirit eyes to see the opportunity above the chaos of current events. Only a person who is trained correctly will be able to capture this time of vast exploits.

Fresh fire will awaken us to the horror of wasting time on silly doctrines and foolish faith. This fire will burn it away and impart a discernment of our time. The flame of God will melt the fear and indecision at our core and forge a "can do" conviction that will carry us to our designated triumph. God loves us but he will replace us if he has to. This unequaled global opportunity for evangelism makes it impossible for the Lord to spare us if we get in His way. He must do whatever it takes to field a proper army.

Let every pastor and leader be warned. The effective church of the near future will not be an entertainment center built by a slick hype; it will be a center of compassion, holiness, and joy. The Lord will not wink any longer at our abuse of charisma. How can He, when untold millions are about to have their first access to the glorious gospel!

CHAPTER TEN

The Lazarus Generation

In many American cities there are hellholes where the ray of hope never shines. The U.S. is home to a wretched generation of violent orphans.

These orphans start out as children subjected to a lethal mixture of shattered families, a cynical culture, and a ready access to guns. Television violence is their only lasting parent.

The jaded, grinding, hollow look in their eyes is a testament of national shame.

The police complain that "youth armies of the night have more firepower than we do." Statistics say that young men in dens of despair have a greater probability of being shot and killed than an American soldier had in Kuwait. There are 70,000 youths in gangs in Los Angeles; experts say their life expectancy is age 19.

Has Satan ever brutalized a generation more? This is why I cry for them. As I cried one night,

God spoke a phrase to me that would alter my whole life. "The Lazarus Generation," God said. "They're coming," God promises. "Who are they?" I wondered.

It is difficult to explain how much turmoil God's voice created in me. I could not imagine such a miracle; I was unable to conceive such an awakening. Yet I knew it was His voice!

To help me, the Spirit led me to Ezekiel 37. Ezekiel had been whisked away to a bluff overlooking a valley of dry bones. God had seen to it that this valley would be the ultimate picture of death.

The Lord asked Ezekiel, "Can these bones live?" Ezekiel gulped and tried to answer; the prophet knew this was a test and he must answer honestly.

My friend Winkie Pratney once said that Ezekiel must have feared that the bones that lay before him were the bones of previous prophets who had failed the test.

Ezekiel answered humbly, "Only you know, O Lord." Although this man of God stood in the very presence of Jehovah, he could not imagine such a miracle.

The Lord issued an amazing command: "Prophesy to these bones that they may live." Ezekiel prophesied, not out of faith but from something greater. What was it?

This cuts to the heart of the most crucial spiritual issue of our day. For years we have glorified faith as the single cause of miracles. Faith is extremely important but another principle can launch us beyond even what our faith can conceive. Ezekiel could not believe or conceive the miracle of the dry bones.

But as it is written: "Eye has not seen, nor ear heard, nor have entered into the heart of man the things which God has prepared for those who love Him." (I Corinthians 2:9 NKJ)

This mighty principle is called *obedience.* When Ezekiel *obeyed* and prophesied, a fierce rattling began. Muscle, sinew, and skin formed out of nowhere. Suddenly there stood an exceedingly powerful army.

Alone in prayer I was confronted and launched out of the confines of my own power to obey!

"Prophesy!" God commanded. Go from the comfortable churches to these hellholes. Prophesy to the crack addict, the teenage prostitute, the young satanists and gang leaders. Prophesy to them *that they may live!*

God will mine treasures out of darkness and out of their graves they will rise to lead the most stunning return to righteousness America has ever seen!

I say again, oh reader . . . there is a Lazarus Generation coming! There will be an army of consuming zeal and a witness so shocking that the most aware churchman could be caught completely off guard.

Who is the Lazarus Generation? They presently are crack dealers, prostitutes, AIDS victims, and gang leaders. They are the elite of Satan's seething, wrenching, "kill America" machine.

In mid-stride, the power of the Holy Ghost will fall on them. Satan will reel in horror to have lost these trophies.

The Lord then warned me that I must be ready to greet and guide these young lions.

First, I am to understand their fanatical love for God. "Gratitude from the grave" is what I call it. What kind of believer do you think a young man would be if he was withered to bone in a bed of an AIDS ward and then suddenly resurrected, cleansed, and baptized in the Holy Spirit?

We had better be ready to train them in true spiritual warfare because they will have a profound intolerance for trivial teaching. They will almost certainly be militant.

If a gang leader is resurrected to Christ, then we must labor to understand his frame of reference. He has controlled city blocks; he has handled automatic rifles; he has risked his life repeatedly.

When he picks up a Bible, his focus will not be emotional healing or self-esteem. He'll ask you where the trigger is and how you fire it. When he reads the Word, he will want to apply it to the taking over of neighborhoods for God.

Over and over I was warned: be ready! Learn to shout from the heart, because they will be shouters. Do not judge them for their appearance.

Lazarus did not have time to change clothes before Jesus raised him from the dead. Lazarus arrived in his grave clothes and so will this generation.

Regularly I go to the Trinity Broadcasting Network studios in Southern California to be with my good friends Paul and Jan Crouch. One of my customs is to go to the phone counselors and greet them. Typically, these beautiful people are quietly ministering to legions who call TBN for help.

On one such occasion I noticed a gaunt young man sitting over in the corner with his back to me. Honestly, his hair looked dead and his garb was a severe contrast to anyone else in the room.

Whereas all the other counselors quietly prayed for the people on the phone, this young man was rebuking Satan in a way I'd never heard! It was one long, unending roar of a lion!

Let me assure you that whomever he was ministering to was delivered! Not only that, but if any bystanders were in the room where this call was going, their demons left too, and I suspect even people walking by lost demons.

For all the warnings God gave me to be ready to shout sincerely, not to judge them, and not to be afraid, let me tell you, I was *not* ready.

This was my first encounter with the Lazarus Generation. This young man turned and looked at me. His face was a mixture of radical new life with the marks of former death. His eyes were pools of fire and purpose and he screamed at me, "Mario Murillo!" I was speechless but he kept screaming. "I was dead! I was lost! I was dying! I was addicted to drugs and I had no hope! Jesus raised me from the dead."

Finally I broke through and screamed right back at him. "I know! I know who you are! You are the Lazarus Generation!"

We embraced and I knew the miracle had already begun.

CHAPTER ELEVEN

We Must Have Fresh Fire
To be Ready
For the Lazarus Generation

I have already seen a great revival blunted and it broke my heart. In the mid-sixties, long-haired hippies began to be wooed by the Spirit to churches all over America.

The Jesus Movement made the cover of "Time" magazine but it never really expressed its full potential of reversing the damage of the 60's.

Two major mistakes kept this wonderful visitation from fulfilling its destiny. The first was the church's over-reaction to appearance. Instead of entreating the young and feeding their hunger and fanning their fire for God, trusting the Spirit to balance them out, the church became the fashion police and didn't see their zeal for God.

A generation already adrift because of their rejection of America's hollow values suffered a second shock to find the church just as superficial.

The second mistake was that many in the Jesus Movement justified their rebellion because of the church's intolerance. The movement fractured into extremes and only a little fruit remained.

We dare not repeat history! The Lazarus Generation is coming and this time we must do what is right; we must do what will allow God to use them and us together.

We need their fiery courage and they need our biblical understanding. They must set us ablaze while we add soundness to their zeal.

Two elements of fire are light and heat. The radical Lazarus Generation will have the heat but with a tolerant, grateful, patient heart, we must provide the light.

Realize that it is now a time for exuberant faith! This includes shouting and exciting worship. There is a need to recognize the intensity of their deliverance, and how radically converted people will express themselves.

I do not condone extreme emotionalism. There is a need for quietness and reverent hymns; however, if we confuse reverence with complacency, we're wrong.

Our flesh may not like the intensity or the volume turned up but there is a time for a war cry. There is a time for shouts of victory.

"Let all things be done decently and in order" is very timely advice.

All expressions of praise must be sincere, Spirit-generated, and full of loving humility. Unless these qualities are present, the worship does not glorify God.

The young, new excited worshipers must also sense when it is right to shout, and correct to be silent.

The Lazarus Generation must be welcomed but also must be brought into balance. But it will not be easy to find this balance; both sides must see it from Christ's viewpoint.

Let us learn from our mistakes in the Jesus Movement. We must not judge by outward appearance. Before we react to purple and green hair and the exotic clothes of the Lazarus Generation, consider how odd some of the hairstyles of Christian television and the church must look to the world.

Next, trust God to soften these converts and soon they'll open up to balance. The dominant emphasis must always be the attitudes of the heart.

As I said before, Lazarus didn't have time to change before he was raised from the dead. He arrived in his grave clothes and so will this generation. But it must be said that these resurrected ones indeed have to grow and be held responsible to grow. They must not become the undisciplined darlings of the church that pastors use as another ploy for growth and popularity.

These converts must not be improperly displayed or given responsibility too soon. With love and care, they must be assimilated into church life without squelching their important zeal.

It is vital for us and them to understand their destiny. They need us and we need them.

Look at an amazing analogy of the vital role of the Lazarus Generation.

David and his men reached Ziklag on the third day. Now the Amalekites had raided the Negev and Ziklag. They had attacked Ziklag and burned it, and had taken captive the women and all who were in it, both young and old. They killed none of them, but carried them off as they went on their way. When David and his men came to Ziklag, they found it destroyed by fire and their wives and sons and daughters taken captive. So David and his men wept aloud until they had no strength left to weep. David's two wives had been captured—Ahinoam of Jezreel and Abigail, the widow of Nabal of Carmel. David was greatly distressed because the men were talking of stoning him; each one was bitter in spirit because of his sons and daughters. But David found strength in the Lord his God. Then David said to Abiathar the priest, the son of Ahimelech, "Bring me the ephod." Abiathar brought it to him, and David inquired of the Lord, "Shall I pursue this raiding party? Will I

overtake them?" "Pursue them," he answered.
"You will certainly overtake them and succeed in
the rescue."   (I Samuel 30:1–8)

How astonishing that David encouraged himself, influenced his grieved army to pursue, and
struck out after the enemy not knowing what
direction to take! David was driven only by a
promise, "Pursue them for you will recover all!"
He rode on, trusting that as he went the
needed piece to the puzzle would be granted.
Out of nowhere came the odd answer:

They found an Egyptian in a field and brought
him to David. They gave him water to drink and
food to eat—part of a cake of pressed figs and
two cakes of raisins. He ate and was revived, for
he had not eaten any food or drunk any water
for three days and three nights. David asked him,
"To whom do you belong, and where do you
come from?" He said, "I am an Egyptian, the
slave of an Amalekite. My master abandoned me
when I became ill three days ago. We raided the
Negev of the Kerethites and the territory belong-
ing to Judah and the Negev of Caleb. And we
burned Ziklag."   (I Samuel 30:11–14)

A dying slave possessed the crucial missing link
to victory! David's compassion and wisdom make
him take time to restore this poor wretched man.

David discerned the slave's role in God's miracle.

David asked him, "Can you lead me down to this raiding party?"   (I Samuel 30:15)

David applied God's provision and won a great victory!

The Lazarus Generation is an indispensable component in our pursuit to restore America. They possess a vital key to victory that Satan didn't realize when he left them for dead!

Without us they may die in the desert; without them we may wander aimlessly, never able to mount a serious attack to take back America.

Because it all boils down to attitudes, only a new igniting of Holy Ghost power will prepare us. We cannot adopt this Lazarus Generation without fresh fire. We need something to burn out the predictability, the cozy church life we have created.

A mighty baptism will free us of hang-ups and prejudices. Only the overflow of the Spirit could have prepared Ananias for his role in the transformation of Saul of Tarsus.

In Damascus there was a disciple named Ananias. The Lord called to him in a vision, "Ananias!"

"Yes, Lord," he answered.

The Lord told him, "Go to the house of Judas on Straight Street and ask for a man from Tarsus named Saul, for he is praying. In a vision he has seen a man named Ananias come and place his hands on him to restore his sight."

"Lord," Ananias answered, "I have heard many reports about this man and all the harm he has done to your saints in Jerusalem. And he has come here with authority from the chief priests to arrest all who call on your name."

But the Lord said to Ananias, "Go! This man is my chosen instrument to carry my name before the Gentiles and their kings and before the people of Israel. I will show him how much he must suffer for my name."

Then Ananias went to the house and entered it. Placing his hands on Saul, he said, "Brother Saul, the Lord—Jesus, who appeared to you on the road as you were coming here—has sent me so that you may see again and be filled with the Holy Spirit." Immediately, something like scales fell from Saul's eyes, and he could see again. He got up and was baptized, and after taking some food, he regained his strength. Saul spent several days with the disciples in Damascus.

(Acts 9:10–19)

This is a textbook example of what we are to do:

(1) Ananias airs his skepticism (verse 13)
(2) The Lord tells him of Paul's destiny (verse 15)
(3) The Lord tells him of Paul's requirements
(4) Ananias obeys God and becomes a vital link for releasing Paul's destiny (verses 17–19)

Again, without the Lazarus Generation, we cannot penetrate America but without us, the Lazarus Generation will not have the scales fall off their eyes to see why they have been called out of darkness.

Finally, what did Jesus order his disciples to do with Lazarus? "Loose him and let him go." A profoundly appropriate command for us now!

We are to loose them and let them go. Moreover, the others in Jerusalem grappled with what to do with the Gentile Christians who were miraculously saved.

It seemed good to the Holy Spirit and to us not to burden you with anything beyond the following requirements: You are to abstain from food sacrificed to idols, from blood, from the meat of strangled animals and from sexual immorality. You will do well to avoid these things.

(Acts 15:28,29)

(1) They said it "seemed good to the Holy
    Spirit and us"
(2) We will not burden you with anything
    beyond these requirements
(3) They issued a clear call to avoid
    immorality

The Lazarus Generation is going to be a lot
of work. But if we put our hearts into it, the
rewards will be beyond calcuation.

PART III

CHAPTER TWELVE

Fresh Fire

*I know the bottom line for me is a fresh baptism in the Holy Spirit—with a "**rushing wind**" freshly billowing the sails of my soul, with a rekindling of "**tongues of flame**" upon my head, and with a "**new language**" of power upon my lips.*
— Dr. Jack Hayford

By now I hope you, like me, possess a deep frustration, an inward turmoil, that makes you dissatisfied with the level of your walk with God! What if I told you that your profound yearning for more had an amazing explanation?

It is very likely that at the root of your agitation of heart is a call by God! Not just any call but a wondrous invitation. You are being drawn and prepared for an event, an impending marvel that will stun our nation with fiery awakening.

This is why you have no use for the rampant shallowness that surrounds you. This is why sometimes you may weep without provocation.

The priorities of so many leave you distressed. You ask, What is our generation's fascination with the trivial?

With each day that passes, your internal desire grows stronger and stronger, begging for expression. Each wave that comes in your spirit tells you that your time on this planet is precious and strategic. You dare not miss your destiny.

These birth pangs are both a warning and an opportunity. The warning is that the charismatic/Pentecostal movement is mired and waning.

It simply breaks the heart of God that we have mutated into a club that conjures up solutions, and lives in opposition to our roots and original purpose.

Jesus said, "You strain at a gnat and swallow a camel." Our camels are being swallowed whole.

If you were to ask the average Christian celebrity what we should do now to revive the movement, here is what you probably would hear, "First, let's oppose gay legislation." Others would offer, "Let's put everyone in cell groups." Still others would prescribe going down to key buildings and shouting at ruling spirits.

What is painful is not that these ideas are

wrong, but they are close enough to being right that they distract us from what we really should do. It takes time to swallow a camel. But what, then, is the gnat that we strain at? It is so basic and obvious that it stings our leaders. We must see that we have relegated the Holy Spirit to *one* baptism when there are *many* subsequent overflowings.

We are a Spirit-filled movement. We must go back and seek a fresh fire. Long before we petition a congressman, lie down in front of an offending clinic, yell at demons, or anything else, we must have a new Day of Pentecost. We must stop the most compelling activities and form upper rooms in every self-respecting, Spirit-filled ministry in America.

This is a solemn warning to everyone who speaks in tongues. We must repent and be *re-baptized* in the Holy Spirit so that we have a legitimate authority to do the true work of God.

Why can't we just admit we need fresh fire? Does the idea of power falling on us threaten the hierarchy because the simplest saint can see the need and go to God directly? Have we lived so long without it that we dread the embarrassment of admitting our need?

Whatever the reason, we are no longer able to justify sparing egos. We are powerless and need a new outpouring of the Spirit.

It is wrong to bask in by-products; we have no

right to engage in feverish activity that has not been fueled by the Holy Spirit.

J. Edwin Orr placed the highest priority on the Spirit being outpoured:

. . . The outpouring of the Spirit effects the reviving of the church, the awakening of the masses, and the movement of uninstructed peoples towards the Christian faith; the revived church, by many or by few, is moved to engage in evangelism, in teaching, and in social action.

The major marks of an Evangelical Awakening are always some repetition of the phenomena of the Acts of the Apostles, followed by the revitalizing of nominal Christians and by bringing outsiders into vital touch with the Divine Dynamic causing all such awakenings . . . the Spirit of God.[6]

As I've said already, you cannot truly want to stop abortions, homosexuality or government corruption unless you cut to the chase by seeing that the most immediately effective and lasting results come from a baptism of fresh fire. By now you can see my primary concern with Spirit-filled Christians: we refuse to return to God to ask for power! My related grievance is that we offend God by basking in by-products and projects fueled by human power.

At the heart of our deception is a fatal misconception of the baptism of the Holy Spirit. We abuse this empowering experience the way many college graduates abuse their diplomas. Graduates often stop learning, assuming that their sheepskin marked an achievement so great that no further education is needed.

Pentecostals presume that their initial baptism of power is a final baptism of power.

When God empowered you to be a witness, it was the first of a *series* of encounters with the Holy Spirit. You must have repeated infusions of power at key points in your life.

Corporately, the church must learn that such returning to God for fresh fire is a reaction to crisis. The pioneers of the Holy Ghost movement earlier in this century recognized this need and called solemn assemblies based on the words of Joel:

Consecrate a fast, call a sacred assembly; gather the elders and all the inhabitants of the land into the house of the Lord your God, and cry out to the Lord.   (Joel 1:14 NKJ)

They realized Joel was right. There has to be a gathering where no one is excused from attending. No one is too young; no one is too old; no one is too smart or too spiritual to be exempted from attending. Joel even required a wedding to be postponed.

Charles Finney referred to times when revival waned and he charged the revival core to press in for renewed power or face the specter of certain death of the movement.

We have replaced the solemn assembly with the seminar. Some roving teacher blows into town and charges a huge amount of money for a one-day, instant-victory seminar.

What is our fascination with quick-fix artists and ideas? Clearly we got it from our television culture, where commercials show deodorants fixing careers and good coffee healing marriages.

We have been conditioned to believe that our spiritual problems will vanish if we could only find that latest technique or secret privilege we have not yet claimed.

We assume that our need is for a new fact, not a new fire.

We should be ashamed! Look at Peter in Acts 3 and 4. He was in the Upper Room; he saw tongues of fire; he tasted the Day of Pentecost! Yet, barely two chapters later he is ordering the church back together for another enduement.

The faith had been banned in Jerusalem because of the miracle to the lame man. Peter saw what we cannot see: only an additional empowerment will help the church answer this threat.

His prayer is a model for how to ask for and receive fresh fire.

"Now, Lord, look on their threats, and grant to Your servants that with all boldness they may speak Your word, by stretching out Your hand to heal, and that signs and wonders may be done through the name of Your holy Servant Jesus." And when they had prayed, the place where they were assembled together was shaken; and they were all filled with the Holy Spirit, and they spoke the word of God with boldness."

(Acts 4:29–31 NKJ)

Peter rightly declared that the threat was from Satan, ultimately against God. In other words, we are under supernatural siege and only supernatural power can answer it.

The next part of his prayer revealed his *motive* for wanting power, and his motive slashes at the heart of what's wrong with us. Peter asked for *boldness to preach the word*. There is not a hint of petition for personal safety, emotional blessing, or lifestyle enhancement. His passion was for the Word of God to have its full impact on the lost and hurting.

He was pleading for miracles that would shatter the chains of the oppressed, thereby releasing even more power for the Word to spread!

Do you see a contrast between praying, "Lord, get me through the week, get me a parking place" and praying, "God, let me have power to boldly speak your word"?

God's power cannot help but overtake that heart that has reduced itself to only wanting the Kingdom advanced.

So it was that fresh fire came again. An earthquake of unity and boldness assured the next era of harvest!

You may have to pray alone or you may be able to gather a core of right-hearted believers. In any case, do what you must do!

Find the place; create the time; fall before God in the discipline of waiting. He is the God who answers by fire. Soon you'll be engulfed and your fears will be ashes. The ensuing sense of purpose will astound you.

Do not wait . . . because the stirring in your heart right now is a signal from Jesus.

CHAPTER THIRTEEN

Charles Finney and Fresh Fire

Preachers have come and gone. Most have had lives that were footprints in the sand. Many brought momentary blaze but left nothing for succeeding generations.

Then again, there are others, legends of ministry, who have bequeathed to us mighty truths and works that live on.

It is urgent for us to discern the factors that mean the difference between faddish fluff and enduring exploits for God.

What was it about these "vessels unto honor" that made them tidal waves of righteousness, that rolled over the evils of their day and enforced the purposes of heaven on millions of souls?

What of John Wesley? He became an earthquake of love. This man gave England a heart attack that awakened compassionate arms to adopt the 30,000 homeless children of London.

The temblor of Methodism expanded to shake several continents into blazing revival.

Consider George Whitfield, who had a voice that was divine mortar fire. Crowds of over a hundred thousand standing outside in snow would hang onto every morsel of gospel he dispensed.

Evan Roberts often wouldn't even preach, just weep. Yet Wales became God's possession under his watch. For nearly 30 years, revival over-flowed this nation and touched the whole world.

About once a year the "Los Angeles Times" prints a defamatory article on Aimee Semple McPherson. Strange . . . when you realize she's been dead nearly 50 years! She wounded Satan so deeply that he is still complaining about her!

These were lives of excellence reminiscent of Samuel. The scriptures say of him, "The hand of God was against the Philistines all the days of Samuel's life. None of his words fell to the ground."

When you read the biographies of these great saints of God, you'll see similarities in courage, vehement prayer, and focused commitment to a vision but you will also see fresh fire.

While lesser preachers were drunk on past achievement, these were never content. They would admit to times when power had declined; they would seek a new infusion of the Holy Spirit.

In my opinion, the greatest American evangelist was Charles Finney. He embodied all the elements of a prophet, an apostle, and a mass evangelist. He did not just birth a ministry but an era.

When he targeted a community with his prayers and preaching, it became ground zero. He took vast numbers of prisoners for Christ and they were converted for life.

But what is most important to this book is that Finney was the major voice to describe a second experience after rebirth that he called "the baptism in the Holy Spirit." He is the grandfather of the Pentecostal movement.

I am indebted to Pastor Jim Reeve of West Covina, California, who earned his Ph.D. at Fuller Seminary in Pasadena, California. His thesis on Charles Finney was a vital aid to me in writing this chapter.

Pastor Reeve said, "In 1845 while reflecting on the causes of the decline in religion and revivals, Finney noted that in more recent years 'fewer of the converts make stable and efficient Christians' and they exhibited 'much less of the Spirit of Christ.' This was due in part, he believed, to the fact that converts were 'not so deeply humbled and quickened and thoroughly baptized with the Holy Ghost as they were formerly.' "

Not only did Finney lament the lack of power but he decried the arrogant assumptions of those who thought one infusion of power was enough for life.

Pastor Reeve again says, "Finney believed that just as one meal did not forever satisfy human physical needs, so one baptism of the Holy Spirit was not sufficient for the spiritual necessities of life. Consequently, new baptisms of the Holy Spirit were needed in order to both maintain and deepen the believer's life of holiness. Since Finney's adoption of the phrase baptism of the Holy Spirit in 1840 he had allowed for more than one experience of being baptized in the Spirit just as he had earlier allowed for more than one experience of being filled with the Spirit. He had noted in 1840 that 'new trials may call for fresh baptisms of the Spirit,' since in this life believers were 'never beyond the reach of sin, never out of danger.' Although it 'behooves' the Christian to 'keep out of temptation's way,' it was a common fact that temptations were sure to come, and 'renewed temptation calls for fresh and more powerful baptisms of the Holy Spirit.' New and fresh baptisms of the Spirit were therefore to be sought and expected so that the Christian could have divine power to overcome even the strongest temptations to sin.

"Finney discovered that new baptisms of the Holy Spirit were needed not only to overcome temptation and maintain the believer's current

state of perfection, but were also needed to enable the Christian to progress in perfection. 'The
Antinomian Perfectionists,' he said, 'supposed
that whoever believes gets so filled as never to
thirst any more.' Quite to the contrary he believed that a truly spiritual person was 'making
still richer attainments in holiness at each rising
grade of progress.' New plateaus of spiritual
attainment were made possible by a baptism of
the Holy Spirit. But even though these spiritual
high places could result in a great sense of triumph, faith, joy, and rest, the appetite for new
and greater 'attainments in holiness' were natural
and unending.

*Subsequently to these scenes will occur other
periods of intense desire for new baptisms of the
Spirit and for a new ascent upon the heights of
the divine life. This is to be the course of things
so long at least as we remain in the flesh, and
perhaps forever . . . Oh, this everlasting progress—this is indeed the blessedness of heaven!*
(Finney, *Gospel Themes*, pp. 412–13)

"So as often as divine power was needed in
order to both maintain and deepen the believer's
life of holiness, God was able and willing to pour
out upon that believer a mighty baptism of the
Holy Spirit.

"It was through deeper and deeper baptisms of the Holy Spirit that people were able to more thoroughly embrace Christ in all of his relations, thereby taking hold of Christ' s divine power and abilities. These fresh baptisms did not make people perfect, rather they enabled already perfect holy believers to progressively make greater attainments in holiness, or, as Finney viewed it, to grow 'from good to better.' "

One factor that drove Finney to the discovery of the need for new baptisms of power was the corruption and shallowness that rose up to choke the awakening in America.

We should let Finney speak to American charismatics! History is repeating itself! Whereas the decline of that revival distressed Finney, I believe that the blatant error and outright sin that now permeates American charisma would cause Finney to fly into a holy rage. While he reacted then as a grieved father, he would behave as an avenging angel today.

But the most telling example is Finney's own experience with fresh fire:

"During the winter of 1843 in Boston, he remembered in his *Memoirs*, his own mind 'was exceedingly exercised on the questions of personal holiness.' In response to prayer, he said, 'the Lord gave my own soul a very thorough overhauling,' which he described as 'a fresh baptism of his

Spirit.' Through this baptism 'it seemed as if my soul was wedded to Christ, in a sense in which I had never had any thought or conception of before.' He subsequently experienced unprecedented 'buoyance and delight in God . . . a steadiness of faith,' and 'a Christian liberty and overflowing love.' All of this, Finney wrote toward the end of his life, was the result of receiving a fresh baptism of the Holy Spirit."

Most charismatics I speak with agree to needing to stay filled with the Spirit. But they assume that a simple act of speaking in tongues for a while achieves "fresh fire." They confuse maintenance with new power.

What we need is a crisis experience every bit as real as the initial baptism of power. Moreover, it is sought with the same deliberate expectation and solemn commitment as the first.

The most convincing example of this is the previously mentioned 4th chapter of Acts. After the man at the Gate Beautiful was miraculously healed, the whole city of Jerusalem was in an uproar.

Peter and John are dragged before the authorities; they are threatened severely and ordered not to teach or preach in the Name of Jesus.

This is the first major challenge the church faces. Satan means to silence them and drive them underground.

Remember something urgent! The Day of Pentecost was in chapter 2 and now in Acts chapter 4, Peter orders them to pray in one accord *all over again*. He is not doubting or diminishing his Pentecostal baptism! On the contrary, he is building upon the boldness acquired in the upper room. He is asking for more of self to be buried in a new wave of Holy Ghost power to face the enemy.

But, you may say, "God is in me in full power." This is not the issue. *Fresh fire is about getting us deeper into God.* Pressing further into His power, being clothed in more of Him, confronting added challenges of spiritual warfare.

Again fresh fire gets us deeper into God who is already in us. The first baptism put us in the Spirit; now a lifetime of reducing self-dependence has begun. Self-dependence is the great enemy of all that the Lord does.

Self is not only conquered by daily choices of surrender, by prayer, by reckoning the work of the cross to ourselves but also by seasons of seeking and receiving new downpours of the Holy Spirit.

Peter orders the prayer meeting and utters a mighty prayer:

"Now Lord, consider their threats and enable your servants to speak your word with great boldness. Stretch out your hand to heal and per-

form miraculous signs and wonders through the name of your holy servant Jesus." After they prayed, the place where they were meeting was shaken. And they were all filled with the Holy Spirit and spoke the word of God boldly.

(Acts 4:29–31)

The added power and boldness they requested was answered in overwhelming abundance.

Are we so blind that we cannot see that we are threatened in America? Are we so proud that we suppose we can do without fresh fire when the disciples sought it so soon after Pentecost?

Do we dare to place ourselves above the legends of God who confessed their need for these deeper baptisms?

There are none so blind, nor a greater threat to revival, than those who hold to the illusion that the charismatic movement in America is intact and needs no infusion of power.

Love and purity are scarce, silliness is rampant, our witness is abandoned, and time is running out.

Already the giddy, smug presumption and pride that marks the death of a movement covers us.

Yet, it need not happen.

A loving, forgiving heavenly Father awaits us. If we discard the garbage and seek the sacred, awesome renewal awaits us.

The signal has come from the throne: *seek fresh fire!* Fire for men and women of God to thunder piercing truth from pulpits, not showy salesmanship in seminars. Fire to burn out the evil in American cities. Fire that builds giant Christians that triumph over end times and move masses by example.

The only person more dangerous than the one who thinks the charismatic movement doesn't need fresh fire is the one who thinks it's the *other* charismatic who needs it.

Say, "*I* need it!"

Now get ready to receive!

CHAPTER FOURTEEN

Fresh Fire:
The Full Effect

We must turn our attention now to the full effect of fresh fire. We need to understand what these infusions do for us. The power of the Spirit is called for in times of *crisis, compromise and opportunity.*

The power of God is revealed when the Person or the work of the Lord is threatened.

A baptism is required when normal efforts fall well short of the fueling charge needed.

A believer can be overcome by desires; a leader can neglect his gift; a movement can compromise its call; prayer can become a ritual. Above all, when God is preparing to open a vast door of opportunity, He seeks to empower us to seize it for Christ's glory.

How can we turn the shallow birth-defective converts in our movement into warriors except by the power of the Holy Spirit? How can we stem the tide of spurious and carnal teachers except by a general baptism of fire that purifies the appetites of charismatics?

Does anyone really believe that this horrible competition and outright contention between "Spirit-filled" churches will go away by having coffee together?

Until these leaders are engulfed in new flames of the Holy Spirit, they will not progress. It is by the Holy Ghost that a preacher's heart is freed of hurt and pride and is restored to the childlike joy of advancing the kingdom with a pure love for the brethren.

The fire will burn off the carnal appendages that have attached themselves to the work of God and choke our life. The fire will awaken appetites for holiness, greatness, and compassion.

Can you simply admit your need for a new overflow of Spirit power? So much frustration will end, so much pain will be prevented. Fresh fire was a recurring theme of Paul the apostle. He himself received it time after time. One very clear example was when the apostle was challenged by Elymas. Paul was suddenly filled with the Spirit.

Then Saul, who also is called Paul, filled with the Holy Spirit, looked intently at (Elymas) and said,

"O full of all deceit and all fraud, you son of the devil, you enemy of all righteousness, will you not cease perverting the straight ways of the Lord? And now, indeed, the hand of the Lord is upon you, and you shall be blind, not seeing the sun for a time."

And immediately a dark mist fell on him, and he went around seeking someone to lead him by the hand. Then the proconsul believed, when he saw what had been done, being astonished at the teaching of the Lord.   (Acts 13:9–12 NKJ)

Now let's look at two prayers of Paul that are unmistakable prayers for deeper baptisms of God.

For this reason I kneel before the Father, from whom his whole family in heaven and on earth derives its name. I pray that out of his glorious riches he may strengthen you with power through his Spirit in your inner being, so that Christ may dwell in your hearts through faith. And I pray that you, being rooted and established in love, may have power, together with all the saints, to grasp how wide and long and high and deep is the love of Christ, and to know this love that surpasses knowledge—that you may be filled to the measure of all the fullness of God.

Now to him who is able to do immeasurably

more than all we ask or imagine, according to his
power that is at work within us, to him be glory
in the church and in Christ Jesus throughout all
generations, for ever and ever! Amen.

(Ephesians 3:14–21)

For this reason, since the day we heard about
you, we have not stopped praying for you and
asking God to fill you with all the knowledge of
his will through all spiritual wisdom and under-
standing. And we pray this in order that you
may live a life worthy of the Lord and may
please him in every way: bearing fruit in every
good work, growing in the knowledge of God,
being strengthened with all power according to
his glorious might so that you may have great
endurance and patience . . .   (Colossians 1:9–11)

These prayers reveal the benefits of these
added outpourings.

Paul speaks of power to do God's work, being
filled with the knowledge of God, mighty
strength, and joy.

This bears out the four characteristics of fire:

(1) It purifies
(2) It fuels
(3) It illuminates
(4) It warms

Let's examine these vital effects of fire:

(1) The purifying work of fresh fire

The most outlandish error of charisma was to overreact to early Pentecostal legalism. We went from no makeup to critical mascara. Holiness is not legalism; legalism is fear and hatred garbed in rules. It judges by outward appearance and afflicts the flesh in order to gain power. This is a corruption of the cross of Christ.

Holiness is born in love! It is the behavior of royalty. True holiness transcends the flesh by gracing the heart with a delight in the commands of the Lord. Holiness is the new affection of a new heart.

Fads in charisma have refused to elevate the believer to a higher plane; it chose, rather, to lower God.

The vehicle for this deception was a misapplication of the doctrine of justification.

Yes, we are justified by the blood of Christ at rebirth, but this dealt directly with what we had *done*. It now takes the daily work of the cross to deal with what we *are*.

Teachers began to espouse the idea that we already had privileges and authority, and were innately blessed because we were born again. We had only to release our inheritance and awaken to the already completed work.

Sanctification dropped out of our vocabulary. Character development was, at best, peripheral.

This error took one further step by redefining success in terms of church size, money, possessions, and visibility, instead of humility, compassion, and a Christlike spirit.

The first touch of fire purifies. False motives for serving God disintegrate; counterfeit faith goes up in smoke. Hay, wood and stubble projects are consumed.

No other work of darkness is more lethal than the insidious pride that lies to us about our true condition.

Samson "wist not that the spirit had left him." He rose up as at other times expecting victory, only to embrace Philistine ridicule and death.

The New Testament Samson was the Laodician church. First, the Spirit exposed their condition.

Because you say, "I am rich, have become wealthy, and have need of nothing"—and do not know that you are wretched, miserable, poor, blind, and naked . . .   (Revelation 3:17 NKJ)

Then fresh fire was prescribed.

I counsel you to buy from Me gold refined in the fire, that you may be rich; and white garments, that you may be clothed, that the shame of your

nakedness may not be revealed; and anoint your
eyes with eye salve, that you may see.

(Revelation 3:18 NKJ)

But what was their greatest danger? They
were in the midst of moral disaster and knew
it not!

This new flame, this next dose of raw Holy
Ghost power, is meant to launch our next level
of conformity to the image of Christ.

The furnace is our friend. We emerge from its
holy work a vessel unto honor. God will find important things for a holy person to do! He will
delight in them; He will joy over them!

Satan's knees just buckled at the thought that
you might surrender to this purifying work of
fresh fire.

(2) Fire illuminates

Stephen had the face of an angel. With an
angry mob poised to pound the life out of him,
a miracle happened. He was filled with the Spirit
and saw Jesus standing at the Father's right
Hand. Death lost its fearful advantage; pain was
rendered inconsequential. The vision of Christ
lifted Stephen to a plane of glory that robbed the
murderers of satisfaction. All that was left for
them to do was to stone the wrapping that he
was discarding.

This was a crisis baptism! It has been the

divine gift of godly warriors and holy martyrs throughout the ages.

Elisha prayed for his fearful associate who could only see the raging charge of 10,000 enemy soldiers. "Lord, open his eyes!" the prophet said.

The servant saw innumerable fiery chariots poised to vaporize any threat to the anointed. *Nothing influences our behavior like our perspective.* What we *see* is the thrust of our life.

Fire carries light. Fresh fire carries divine light. Scales fall off our view of things, and to see rightly is to empower to live rightly.

The fire which is from God awakens the nominal believer. They are elevated to being "seated with Christ in heavenly places." What an astonishing difference when you gaze at life from this vantage point!

You make excellent choices. The frowning problems of your life become insignificant compared to the vista that floods your soul! The walls of doubt become speed bumps.

You can't compromise because you see the glory that will be revealed in you. You walk holy because you see it is making you like Christ. You take hold of mighty projects because you can see the completion of them.

Your passion for the lost becomes gigantic because you see their dreaded state. You are given the gift of sight! Eyes of the Spirit! By this fire's light you become a mighty warrior.

As I said earlier, how significant that as David's mighty men were being described for their special strength, the weapon of the men of Issachar was "They knew the times and what Israel should do." Their perception was their weapon!

So will the Spirit light give us sight in this present darkness. We will forgive our enemies, for we see their offenses from heavenly ramparts. We work with fellow soldiers because the vision of unity pervades us. We march with swords drawn to the very throat of Satan because we see his doom is sure.

(3) Fire fuels

"According to the power that works in us."

Change requires power. You may want to change; you may possess the will to change and the opportunity. Yet the desired alteration escapes you. We are prisoners of a force greater than we know!

Even when all the elements for transformation seem present, nothing will happen unless a vital ingredient is present.

It is that irreplaceable element that converts good intentions into resurrection living. It is that fuel that fires up the engine of lasting change.

It is a wonder that the same fire that can destroy can be utilized as fuel. "If the same spirit which raised Christ from the dead dwell in you, it will quicken your mortal body."

"For it is God who works in you both to will and to do his good pleasure."

Sometimes progress is so hard to come by that radical action must be taken. The inner man must be jump started; re-emerging lusts must be overpowered; extra force must be applied when the weight of daily life threatens our advancement.

The fresh fire experience is a power surge that animates failing limbs, weak knees, and a faltering spirit. But this fuel is so much more! The fire that I speak of imparts the energy to do the will of God!

Saul cowered before the destiny Samuel described for him. "How can I do this thing?" Saul asked. Hear the prophet's resolute reply, "The Spirit of the Lord will come upon you and you will be changed into another man!"

Fresh fire is no mere "clean up your act" encounter. Here is the fuel to fire up the engine.

Was it this enduement of **dunamis** that Daniel prophesied? "Those who know their God will be strong and carry out great exploits." (Daniel 11:32)

Let the crowd become a warrior and the faint

a force. Let us embrace our launching from mere living to multiple triumphs. Here is higher octane for a higher calling.

(4) Fire warms

The joy of the Lord is our strength (Nehemiah 8:10). A lifetime of study will not reveal the weight of this statement!

Joy from God is our great distinction from the world. The pagan must have right circumstances to have right feelings.

Remove possessions from the world of pagans and their life stops. For the lack of God they are bound to outer life support systems for satisfaction.

Curiously, the church forgets her first love so easily! You can tell when the level of the "oil of gladness" is low; it shows in the preaching.

When pulpiteers heap perks onto the gospel to make it palatable to secular ears, it is because their own vision of Jesus has been tarnished. He is no longer all they need, so He is no longer all that they prescribe.

The reward of salvation is Jesus. He alone is the treasure in the field; He is the person of wonder that "bids our sorrows cease."

He spoke and our parking lot became a garden; how soon we forget!

When Paul said, "I have learned in whatsoever state I am therewith to be content," it was the fire of joy that elevated him to a higher awareness than his standard of living.

This well in us is our greatest protection. It keeps God's commands in their proper context: *light* and *reasonable*!

Tell me if there is anything worse than the coldness of modern life. Natural love is gone; children are deemed disposable; and the grind of the workplace chews up hope.

The Godless man has no refuge, no rationale to keep trying. Daily they toy with various progressive forms of suicide.

The joy of the Lord is a force field that insulates against the destructive, draining spirit of this age. A layer of love keeps the infection of despair off us.

"Godliness with contentment is great gain," said the Apostle Paul. Perhaps the greatest blend in a saint would be the combined zeal, flat-out crush-on-Jesus spirit of a young convert and the solid wisdom, strength and experience of a veteran warrior!

These then are the four major effects that Fresh Fire will have on us.

CHAPTER FIFTEEN

Fresh Fire:
Now Receive It!

Have you made up your mind? Have you brushed off the cobwebs of mediocre charisma?

It's normal at times to feel an odd mixture of dread and excitement! Your flesh is fearful because it knows it's about to be driven back to proper subjection. Your spirit, however, is soaring in anticipation of increased power.

Relief will bathe your soul once you have firmly decided not to accept a half answer to your spiritual condition.

What you crave is a full measure of fire, a deeper baptism. You want a permanent break from nominal living. You do not want to be sidelined during the next wave of God on America.

Above all, you are convinced that God has more for you than what you imagined.

So now doubts are gone, excuses are buried and you will accept nothing less than fresh fire.

This is the first step. Renounce even the hint of compromise! Accept no substitute. Do not pursue merely a safe dose of God.

In your proclamation of the need for fresh fire, you have concluded that this is not a case of routine maintenance or of turning over a new leaf or of breaking habits by will power.

You have discerned the issue is at the heart. You have resolutely decided that a light swoon will not do. You want a launching of Holy Ghost power! As at the first, you want **dunamis** at the core of your being that will radiate out of every member.

Now you become a seeker of God. He rewards them that diligently seek. James warns us against being double minded. We are not to be guilty of hidden agendas or escape valves. We are asking in order to receive, not to go through a ritual to look spiritual.

You are here to stay because you want the treasure of fresh fire. You don't want the old nature to reassert itself. You don't want your forward progress hindered any longer. Above all, you don't want to sink on the deck of this Titanic of charismatic fluff.

Not only are you determined to seek; you want to seek correctly. To do so means to hark back to when you first received the baptism in the Holy Spirit. You came as a child, trusting the Lord's mercy and believing in His desire to baptize you. Then you waited worshipfully in His presence. Do it again; come in that attitude again.

And I say to you, Ask, and it will be given to you; seek, and you will find; knock, and it will be opened to you. For everyone who asks receives, and he who seeks finds, and to him who knocks it will be opened. (Luke 11:9,10 NKJ)

You may need to tarry, and focused tarrying is a lost art! Some early Pentecostals reduced tarrying to legalistic torture. They believed you had to suffer to earn Holy Ghost power. On the other hand, many charismatics have cheapened the act of waiting and the results are equally disastrous.

One extreme frustrates the seeker and adds unwarranted pain to waiting on God. The spirit is hindered because He is ready to give us the gift but we are too preoccupied with self abasement to receive it.

The other extreme is instantism. The seeker is instructed to babble a few syllables and is excitedly told that they've "got it." This has aborted many from truly getting the Holy Spirit baptism. The convert is sent home with a synthetic experience without truly encountering the power of God.

True tarrying is a marriage of expecting and persevering. You must see the vision of Christ as

the willing baptizer and yourself as the one quali-
fied to receive, not because of your worthiness
but because of His righteousness in you.

You are set for the long run because you know
your waiting is a process of love, not punishment.
Gratitude fuels your patience. Here is a divine
gift you don't deserve that promises to enrich
your life and you are overcome by the goodness
of God.

So, you wait, expecting at any moment that
fire may fall, but if it doesn't, you have nowhere
else you'd rather be. And nothing else you could
do would be more important, anyway.

God signals the end of your quest by baptizing
you. And again, as before, you are not seeking
tongues. Do you remember your first Pentecost?
It wasn't tongues that impressed you most about
the baptism in the Holy Spirit! It was the Al-
mighty God Himself! The same sense of Jesus
will pervade you again, as the first time.

We must navigate the crucial act of waiting on
God with care! Again, determine to balance your
pursuit with an equal measure of faith to receive
at any moment and with an attitude of being
willing to wait.

Fresh fire can be sought privately or corporately. God honors both. You may be driven by
the Lord to the secret closet of prayer. Or He
may summon a church to a solemn assembly.

What could be more loving for a pastor to do than to organize a fresh fire prayer night patterned after Peter in Acts 4?

Let the pastor be bold! Announce it as a night where the Holy Spirit himself will run the service!

Let the Body come before the Lord saying, "We have come for fresh fire." He who is God will answer by fire! Hallelujah!

What a mighty moment when we cry out as humble children to Him who will not fail to answer! Boldness will be increased and wicked influences will die.

Our great enemy is our schedule. Yes, our lives are complicated. Time is very scarce; routine is a bully that intimidates us into accepting an inferior life.

But remember, this is God calling. He considers our obligation; He knows the daily burden, yet He calls. If He calls, He will create the way of escape from our rat race to His upper room.

The next enemy will be revealed as you contend in prayer. The flesh and its toxic residue built up over time, unbeknownst to us, and will rear up and agitate you. Suddenly you'll feel like bolting from the place of prayer. Keep your eyes on the prize. Weather this attack and you'll reach rich fulfillment.

God deals with us for our good. When He surfaces a secret sin, it is to free us. The Spirit of God may even parade a band of unfinished matters. Unforgiveness may be anchoring your soul to second-rate living.

Some of these issues are resolved alone, between you and God, while others will require going and making it right.

But what is your greatest enemy in your quest for fresh fire? The arrogant, smug presumption that your need is not urgent because you are already Spirit filled.

This blind assumption is the lethal swill of flaky charismatics. These superficial believers are the Hemlock Society of our movement. They'll gladly assist you in committing spiritual suicide!

These are the groupies who chase self-conceited teachers, who spout fantasy-laden promises and hollow victories. Their high-sounding words will lead us on field trips through futility. Remember that their teachings build no character, attack no meaningful demonic targets, and do not carry the gospel to the lost.

Separate yourself from the silly. Face your own need for power, real power, holy power, power that is the deepest dread of Satan.

Do you vividly recall your first baptism? Now, as then, you will be transformed and feeble prayers will become torrents of intercession.

Old habits, like the bowstrings that bound Samson, will break like yarn touching fire.

The cry of the warrior within will erupt like a volcano. Climb above the stupor of this generation. Go now and find the place to seek this next enduement.

Wait there in expectant obedience. Fresh fire is about to fall on you!

Select Bibliography

1. Richard Lovelace, DYNAMICS OF SPIRITUAL LIFE (Downers Grove, Illinois: Inter-Varsity Press), p. 245.
2. Tommy Barnett, PORTRAITS OF VISION (Nashville, Tennessee: Thomas Nelson Publishers), p. 115.
3. Richard Lovelace, DYNAMICS OF SPIRITUAL LIFE (Downers Grove, Illinois: Inter-Varsity Press), p. 209.
4. R. Arthur Mathews, BORN FOR BATTLE (Robesonia, Pennsylvania: Overseas Missionary Fellowship), p. 109.
5. Richard Lovelace, DYNAMICS OF SPIRITUAL LIFE (Downers Grove, Illinois: Inter-Varsity Press), p. 247.
6. J. Edwin Orr, EVANGELICAL AWAKENINGS IN SOUTHERN ASIA (Minneapolis, Minnesota: Bethany Fellowship, Inc.), p. vii.

Mario Murillo has written several other books, including the best seller CRITICAL MASS. For information on other books, cassettes, video-cassettes, or to receive Mario's monthly newsletters, please write to:

MARIO MURILLO MINISTRIES
P.O. Box 5027
San Ramon, CA 94583